TOYO
ITO

The Kassler Lectures

Other books in the series include:
R. Buckminster Fuller: World Man

Publication is made possible in part by a grant
from the Barr Ferree Foundation Fund, Department
of Art and Archaeology, Princeton University.

TOYO ITO

FORCES OF NATURE

JESSIE TURNBULL
EDITOR

PRINCETON UNIVERSITY
SCHOOL OF ARCHITECTURE

AND

PRINCETON ARCHITECTURAL PRESS
NEW YORK

CONTENTS

PREFACE

Princeton University School of Architecture has had the great fortune since 1966 of hosting the Kassler Lectures. Established in memory of longtime Princeton instructor and critic Kenneth Stone Kassler, the endowed series periodically brings the leading architects and thinkers of the day to speak to students at the school. No period in the series' history has been more fruitful in doing so than the tenure of Dean Stan Allen, who brought a succession of international architectural luminaries onto the Princeton campus to talk about their work.

The idea to transform the Kassler Lectures into a series of books—although in the air from the very start—also solidified under Dean Allen's leadership, following the enthusiastic response in 2009 to Toyo Ito's lecture. Startling in its simplicity of format, clarity of rhetoric, and richness of visual imagery, the very nature of Ito's presentation recommended its publication.

Stan Allen was instrumental in paving the way for the series of publications, and together we shaped this volume to flesh out the discourse surrounding Ito's most recent work. His essay bridges the architect's earliest project, the White U house, with the (sadly unrealized) Berkeley Art Museum and Pacific Film Archive, which Ito had carefully unpacked, along with two other important works, in his Kassler lecture. Ito's 1978 essay "The Reflection of the *Sacred* in the *Profane* World" was selected for inclusion, first, in light of its close reading of the White U, but second, because of its careful analysis of architecture within the physical and social contexts of the city. These latter themes are fully developed, and the more sociopolitical aspects of Ito's work explored, in Julian Worrall's essay, which incorporates excerpts from a recent conversation between the author and the architect.

Any book documenting the recent work of Toyo Ito would be incomplete without considering the catastrophic effects of the 2011 Tohoko earthquake and tsunami. We are grateful to include an early sketch for "Home for All," a communal living project initiated by Ito, which is now under construction in the Tohoko region of Japan. The title of this book, <u>Toyo Ito: Forces of Nature</u>, projects the connotation that Ito's architecture responds to forces within a broadly understood environment; flows of digital information, social ecologies and constructs, as well as natural forces and even disasters.

Many people contributed great time and effort to realizing this project. The graphic designer Alice Chung of Omnivore created a compact and sophisticated package for this volume, responding graciously along the way to every graphic suggestion. Nancy Eklund Later of Princeton University School of Architecture Books has been indispensable with her publishing expertise and impeccable scheduling. Publisher Kevin Lippert, Senior Editor Megan Carey, and the design and production team at Princeton Architectural Press have made a welcome home for the project on its prodigious list.

While we were in the process of putting the content of this book together, Dan Claro, the resourceful and insightful curator of Princeton University School of Architecture's Visual Resources Collection, uncovered the original manuscript of the inaugural Kassler Lecture, delivered by R. Buckminster Fuller. It was totally obvious that this should become the starting point for the book series, and so <u>Toyo Ito: Forces of Nature</u> is published as the second volume in the Kassler Lectures series.

This book could never have happened were it not for the kindness of Toyo Ito and the endless patience and generosity of Miki Uono, the architect's secretary, who answered our many questions and requests promptly, knowledgeably, and positively. Our sincere gratitude and thanks go out to them both.

TOYO ITO'S PATIENT SEARCH

STAN ALLEN

If anything is described by an architectural plan, it is the nature of human relationships, since the elements whose trace it records—walls, doors, windows and stairs—are employed first to divide and then selectively to re-unite inhabited space.

—Robin Evans

The big problem is then how to preserve the sense of floating in a space with no exterior.

—Toyo Ito

Le Corbusier famously wrote that creation in architecture is a "patient search."[1] Among architects working today, only Toyo Ito approaches Le Corbusier's restless creativity. On at least three occasions over his long career, he has designed buildings that simply rewrite the rules of the game—definitive statements of architectural principles that become new points of reference for other architects. Although he is a thoughtful writer, his contributions are not discursive. His buildings do not exemplify concepts enunciated elsewhere: it is the power of the built artifacts themselves that provokes our reassessment. They establish a state of play between *before* and *after*. It is simply impossible, for example, to think about domestic space in the same way after his 1976 White U house, arguably the most radical house of the twentieth century. His Sendai Mediatheque (designed in 1995 and completed in 2000) culminated a decade-long preoccupation with the effects of emergent digital technologies on architecture, which he has called "the body of electronic modernism."[2] Finally, his 2007 Tama Art University Library simultaneously sums up a decade of structural experimentation as it

demolishes many of our conventional notions about the space of the library.

Although the delicacy and restraint of his buildings feels innately Japanese, one of the astonishing things about Ito's work is the way in which he constantly refers back to Western classical traditions, taking them apart from the inside out. The filigree of arches at the Tama Art Library, for example, would seem to recall the proto-historicist work of the 1960s, when late-modern architects such as Philip Johnson and Edward Durrell Stone sought to soften the polemical force of the new through classical reference. The result at the time was paper-thin and decorative, a kind of classical appliqué over a lightweight modern framework. But the arches at the Tama Art Library are not a quotation of classical form: they are devices for activating space. They vary in size, and their profiles are not classically half-round but elliptical. They have nothing to do with the postmodernist use of the arch as an applied sign. Instead they register an interpenetrating spatial form, which owes something to the classical idea of the library but can no longer be represented as a solidly enclosed space.

The gently convex perimeter of Ito's library, for example, suggests space beyond the limits of the building. Destabilized by the sloping floor, the visitor registers the library as an elastic void tracing out the vectors of the program, mirroring the dynamic, interlinked quality of information today. The moving spectator perceives

that just when you think Ito has exhausted a certain line of inquiry, he is capable of surprising everyone (including himself). The rest of the discipline spends ten years catching up. This is the measure of Ito's creative intelligence. Despite his fascination with digital media and new social formations, Ito, who has been building for more than forty years, knows that architecture is a slow medium with a very specific social agency. It is structurally tied to institutions that are themselves conservative and slow to change. Nevertheless, for Ito it remains both possible and necessary to renew architecture through this long cycle of critique, reassessment, and invention.

the interpenetrating profiles in parallax, more Richard Serra than Robert Venturi.[3] Finally, the dimension and material quality of the arches erases their traditional representational function. Constructed from steel plates encased in concrete, they are impossibly thin: they could never operate in compression, as a classical arch does. Your eye tells you that they are almost too thin to stand by themselves. In fact, the arched form is almost accidental, the result of carving out the void space rather than a reference to the arch's supporting function. With this array of devices, Ito does not so much attack or confront the classical tradition as accept and redirect its persistent impulse toward stability and the representation of function.

This pattern, of an extended career marked by the periodic appearance of paradigm-shifting projects, suggests

Of the three buildings discussed here, it is the Sendai Mediatheque that has, perhaps deservedly, received the most attention. Here Ito definitively reconfigured the slab and column organization of Le Corbusier's Dom-ino-type form. For the first time, the Mediatheque takes into account not just structure but all of architecture's other imperatives: movement, fire safety, vertical transport, and mechanical and environmental engineering. Up to this point, the conventional approach had been to address each new need with a new system, thus multiplying the number of elements. In Ito's proposal, the hollow columns perform multiple functions, allowing him to reduce the number of elements. Paradoxically, this enables him to recuperate the elemental dialogue of the horizontal space of occupation with its vertical support, this time with the idea of "support" enlarged to include more than mere structure.

At Sendai, Ito brilliantly demonstrated the capacity of simple rules to produce complex architectural and social effects. Architecture, as much as it is a tectonic support, is also the creation of a localized artificial atmosphere that connects

in turn to larger information networks. It is in these more ephemeral aspects of building that architecture can reshape social interaction today. The Mediatheque suggests that, in an increasingly dematerialized social milieu, the physical space of encounter that architecture provides still has meaning. It is the architecture itself

that deserves rethinking under these new conditions. Unlike Reyner Banham, who in the mid-1960s imagined the house reduced to a plastic bubble inflated by air-conditioning output, Ito does not turn away from architecture or dissolve its physicality but instead revises and enlarges its capacity as a social technology under modern conditions of information drift.[4]

If the Sendai Mediatheque is, in both its architectural form and its social ambition, outward-looking, the White U is its opposite: an intimate, inward-looking space. Not only is the architecture organized around an inner court with a nearly blank street wall, the program itself is deeply private. It is impossible not to invoke the history of the house, designed and built for Ito's sister and her two young children, whose husband and father had recently succumbed to cancer. Enveloped over time by vines, it was finally demolished in 1997. Only an architecture that is honest and subtle in its architectural effects could adequately address such an extreme personal narrative. Here, Ito's architectural precision does not disappoint. He describes how subtle architectural shifts can revise the way a form is perceived: "As I displaced the entrance from the symmetry axis toward the edge, the interior of the building lost that hard aspect of the room conferred by linearity and the U became a white ring."[5] The courtyard, due in part to its blank walls, is more than a void defined by the perimeter: it is a palpable, thick space. It anchors the composition. This is reinforced by the inward slope of the roof, which seems to focus all of the

space's continuity: a tangent fold opens a generous window in the blank courtyard wall and situates the dining table; a modest vestibule accommodates passage from the street; and a staggered corner and half-circle arc navigate the transitions between the spaces. As Alain Robbe-Grillet once observed about Franz Kafka's writings, "The hallucinatory effect derives from their extraordinary clarity and not from mystery or mist. Nothing is more fantastic, ultimately, than precision."[6] In the White U, this translates to a minimal number of parts perfectly calibrated between balance and imminent discord or collapse.

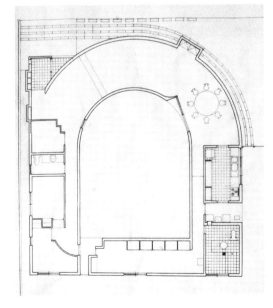

space toward the empty courtyard and its floor of black soil. The plan organization turns its back on the street. The asp-like half-round, which would normally terminate an axis of movement, becomes the front instead. This means that the symmetry of the space is broken by the entrance, and at the back of the site, the "U" is only partially closed, giving a certain sense of incompleteness and contingency. The incidents of occupation are minor interruptions to the

14

In one of his earliest essays, Robin Evans points out that it is only in the nineteenth century that the corridor was fully integrated into domestic space planning. In the palaces and villas of the Renaissance and beyond, space was organized as a "matrix of connected rooms," always making it necessary, when moving through the house, to traverse one room to reach another.[7] The division of private and public space (or served and servant space, as Louis Kahn would later describe it) coincided with the emergence of the middle class. The simultaneous flattening and stratification of social hierarchy was reflected in the partitioning of domestic space into private and public realms. The White U, on the other hand, is nothing but corridor, a restless space of movement and transition. This suggests a space of transience, of impermanence, and at the same time a projection of the private realm of the corridor into the public realm of the house. It is a house without any conventional collective spaces, such as a living room or sitting room. An early plan drawing strategically excludes the

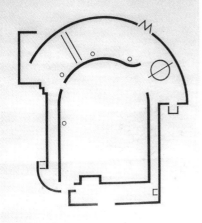

spaces of inhabitation—only the corridor remains. Ito describes the house as a "uniform tubular space." "All openings were closed," he writes, "and the natural light beams falling sparsely from above strengthened the impression of an underground labyrinth. At the same time the white summoned more white, and the curved surfaces enhanced their own curvature."[8] It is worth remembering that before Westerners brought the black frock coat to Japan in the nineteenth century, white was the color of mourning. Despite this, and even despite the metaphor of the house as an underground space, the white surfaces suggest not heavy emotion but lightness and delicacy, even optimism.

European modernism embraced transparency and opened the space of the house out to the landscape. For the architects of the early twentieth century, this exteriority had a polemical force. The plush interior had developed in the nineteenth century as a comforting retreat from the hard reality of the modern metropolis. *Interiority* implied a withdrawal into individual subjectivity, politically suspect and artistically bankrupt. By contrast, the modernist interior—flooded with light—minimized the distinction between interior and exterior. Its subject was thrust out into the world to confront the hard realities of modernity head-on. But Adolf Loos, who so often turned convention on its head, pursued an alternative approach. He wrote that the exterior of the house must be mute, and the house should only reveal itself from within.[9] For Loos this translated to the complex interlocked spaces of the *raumplan* and the strategic use of rich materials like marble and exotic woods, whose figured surfaces provided an intrinsic ornament to the space. Loos imagined a new, fundamentally modern interiority, in which media and emergent information technologies blurred the boundary between interior subjectivity and public collectivity.[10] The spaces of the White U are highly restrained, and there is none of Loos's sectional interlock: their fullness is invested in surface effects rather than the result of carefully calibrated effects of light and space. Ito, now operating fully within the logic of the Information Age, radicalizes Loos's split between interior and exterior, dissolving both into a kind of white noise: a signal without a message.

Ito has described the elements of the house as "light" and "soil," a confrontation

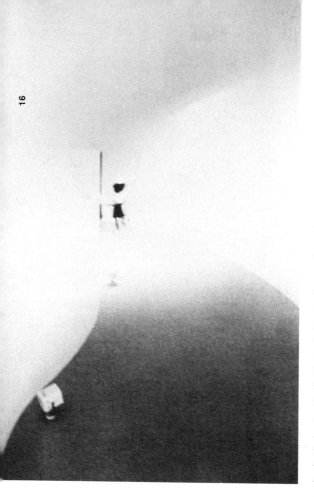

wrote, for example, that "windows like cracks in the ceiling would please me."[12] Everything about the house, from its blank exterior and palpable emptiness, to the sensation of being underground, to the ghostly images of the children in photographs of the time, reinforces this intensely personal narrative. In his essay "Architecture" of 1910, Loos wrote, "The work of art aims at shattering man's comfortable complacency. A house must serve one's comfort."[13] He argues that art and architecture have fundamentally different tasks. The artist has an obligation to challenge received ideas and imagine alternative futures, whereas the architect must be attentive to the needs of the present and the collective memory of the past. For Loos, "Only a small part of architecture belongs to art: the tomb and the monument."[14] In the case of the White U, the singular narrative of the house demanded a more intense and personal response, one that sanctions Ito's foray into the territory of art. This does not contradict Loos so much as suggest that in this house the functions

between light and dark, nature and culture. He writes that he was searching for a "whole, stable form," a kind of "independent utopia" that could reconstitute the idea of a family in the face of great loss.[11] But he also understood that this utopia—precisely in order to fulfill its role in rebuilding the family—could not be false or conciliatory. Ito's sister

微妙的に フラットスラブ、海草のような柱、ファサードのスクリーン
へる要素だけし ピラ下に発現する。それぞれのエレメントを構造的に
どんどん slim し シンプルに する ことに 努力をあげる。これはスラブすべて void にしたい!!

ファサードのスクリーン
コの字型の（里成）のみ
（里成、程度の内）
フレームは14449?

スラブは想定から抜く
フラント Floor Hight
のラシグル

steel pipe へ細かくする。
もしくは
鉄骨柱に
交えあわせたい。
?

コア、沿うなど
とどこを含む

底 ← ガラスシャフト
スラブのなかが void から 変更しようとって
底にする

23. Jan '95
Toyo Ito

of memory associated with the tomb and the monument are never far away. With the White U, Ito has fused the introverted idea of the house as private refuge with the collective function of memory and public mourning. This is what elevates the house from a private matter to a public testament. At the same time, considering the fugitive character of memory, it is only fitting that the story of the house ends with its demolition. To preserve the object artificially, apart from the life of its inhabitants, would be an empty gesture.

In the White U, the plan is still the primary organizing device. In most of Ito's work since that time, it is secondary. At Sendai, section is decisive, and at Tama, a fully developed three-dimensional spatial matrix is in play. This certainly owes something to Ito's extended collaboration with the engineer Mutsuro Sasaki, who also made decisive contributions to the design of the Sendai Mediatheque. In conversation with Ito, Sasaki has proposed that contemporary developments in structure can be traced back to two figures: Mies van der Rohe and Antonio Gaudí. The infinite horizontal of Mies implies a minimal structure, while Gaudí's figured form anticipates what Sasaki calls "flux" structure.[15] In that same conversation, Ito describes the Mediatheque as a series of cave-like holes drilled through a compact volume. For Ito, this dialectic between the regularity of the structure and the worm-like voids speaks to the

dispersed quality of information in the Digital Age. This concern persists at Tama, where the program is more conventional but marked (as is the program of any contemporary library) by the erosion of solidity that digital information implies. Seen this way, Tama might be understood as a series of *horizontal* cavelike spaces drilled through a compact volume, with its attenuated walls taking the place of the thin slabs at Sendai.

An anecdote from the design process confirms this account. Ito had recently completed the Crematorium in Kakamigahara with Sasaki and was tending toward a similar solution, with a smoothly curving structure. In the early design studies for the library, Ito's office approximated these continuous surfaces with cardboard templates. Looking at the model, Ito realized that there was no

need to literally complete the surfaces. At Kakamigahara smooth structure yields smooth space; the effect is stunning, but the technical investment is disproportionate. The symmetry of support and affect does not produce a significant transformation. At Tama, what happens is more complex: a segmented structure yields a smooth space. Referring to the persistence of the image on the retina, which creates continuous movement out of still images in cinema, Gilles Deleuze writes, "cinema does not give us an image to which movement is added, it immediately gives us a movement-image."[16] At Tama, the spatial experience of the moving spectator smooths out the intervals between the striated architectural elements to a similar effect: not of literal movement but the taut energy of a body in motion—a *movement-image*. The

discovery here is that flux structure does not need to be literally smooth; instead, the design of the interval itself, and the relationship of the parts, imparts smoothness to the segmented structure.

Ito further developed these ideas in the project for the Berkeley Art Museum and Pacific Film Archive (BAM/PFA), designed in 2008. Berkeley represents an intensification and internalization of the structural and spatial ideas explored at Tama. If today's library suggests a fluid information space that extends past the boundary of a single building, the program of the art museum neces-

sarily entails protection and enclosure. Beyond the simple need for vertical walls to accommodate the display of art, the museum needs to house the works and establish an autonomous identity for the institution. These requirements are incompatible with the idea of pure flux. The museum program alternates between stasis (the slow contemplation of works) and movement (the flow of spectators through the collection). The dialogue that had previously animated Ito's works—between the delicacy of the Miesian volume and the figural space of information—takes on a very specific meaning at Berkeley. The contemporary rethinking of interiority, the "sense of floating in a space with no exterior" that

Ito first explored in the White U, returns here in another form.

The Swiss architect Valerio Ogliati contends that architects are either adders or dividers. The Mediatheque is clearly an additive project, a system of horizontal floors held up by hollow, woven columns. The walls at Tama divide space, although the spectator's movement stitches it back together. Berkeley is perfectly calibrated between the two. Ito's proposal is a compact, three-story cubic volume that fills the given site. It imparts a sense of urban density to its loose, campus-based context. The registration of the thin slab edges suggests a simple stacking operation (as at Sendai), but here, for programmatic reasons, the perimeter is closed. The elevation is a snapshot of the sectional organization. At Sendai, Ito lightly enclosed a fragment of continuous space—punctuated by hollow columns—into which all of the necessary services were packed. At Berkeley, the space appears dense, and thicker. The convex profiles suggest pressure from within. It is as if the lacy columns of Sendai have solidified and swelled to the edges of the site, spilling the services out to create a tightly packed cellular matrix. The effect is one of arrested motion and potential energy, perfectly mirroring the programmatic mix and urban aspirations of the project.

In plan, the site is divided into a simple four-by-four matrix, which yields rectangular programmatic modules. Any grid can be seen simultaneously as accumulation and division, and Ito plays up this ambiguity, moving from closed cells at the lower level (with pedestrian passages in between) to a dense weave of galleries up above. There is no distinction between served and servant spaces, and there are no corridors. The more primitive "matrix of connected rooms" described by Evans reappears, but Ito does not default to the conventional *enfilade* strategy so often employed in museum design. Instead, the walls sway and bulge and loop back on themselves. This undulation creates interstitial spaces for passage and a spatial rhythm as the viewer moves between concave and convex spaces. Renderings show both the enclosed galleries and the passages utilized as exhibition space. This serves to confound the sense of

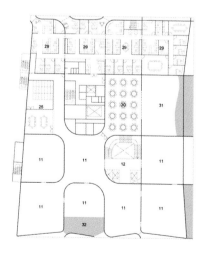

2F plan

3F plan

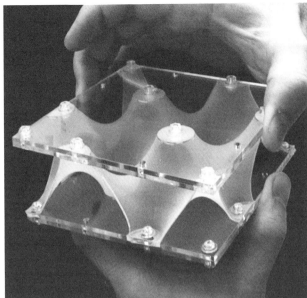

on the lightness of Tama, the Berkeley project is part of another line of inquiry in Ito's work—that of elastic, three-dimensional cellular projects such as the Taichung Metropolitan Opera House (under construction and expected to be complete in 2013) and the Ghent Forum for Music, Dance and Visual Culture (2005). Like the museum,

public and private, unpacking the "white cube" model of the conventional gallery. The plan language oscillates along multiple readings: the grid as a fragment of continuous space; an infinite line looping back on itself to enclose space; and a collection of living cells captured at the instant of division.

The sense of arrested movement in the BAM/PFA is not limited to the plan. The cell walls billow and sway in section as well, and there are openings in the elevation that appear as cuts, the result of the swelling form being sliced by the perimeter of the site. Invisible currents of movement become visible at the moment they come in contact with the envelope of the building. As much as it follows

these are introverted programs, where the audience's attention is collectively focused on the performance. The museum program is more dispersed: it needs to create at once a series of inwardly directed spaces of contemplation and a series of outwardly directed spaces of public engagement. Ito alternates between the two with exquisite subtlety. He does so not by adjusting the essential language of the proposal but by teasing out a latent flexibility in the apparently static, grid-like organization. And, as is so often the case with Ito, these deviations from the norm are never overt. They trust in nuance and suggestion. This sense of immanent change projects a new idea of the institution, suspended between inside and outside, whole and fragment, finality and revision.

The delicacy of the tectonic language reinforces this sense of institutional provisionality. Where one would conventionally expect weight and solidity, Ito answers with lightness, which for him is the ever-present shadow of the flux of information today. The architecture is pushed right up to the edge of dematerialization, with the full knowledge that it can never actually be dematerialized. Instead, the heavy is made light. But the lightness of this architecture is not a lightness that works against the hardness of technical laws: it works tactically to achieve effects of lightness by architectural (as opposed to purely technical) means. It is a lightness of tectonic precision, a lightness of software as opposed to one of hardware.[17]

In the work of some architects, like Rem Koolhaas at OMA, the force of the project as an idea outweighs the need for its construction: OMA's project for the Jussieu Library, for example, has had an enormous impact on the field despite its never having been built.[18] By contrast, Ito's work only reveals its richness and complexity through construction—not because the architect revels in materiality, but for just the opposite reason. It is only in built form that the subtlety of his dematerialized relationships—the play of light and space activated by the inhabitant—and the sophistication of his tectonic solutions become fully evident. His work is not so much about making the nature of materials visible as it is about material

transformation: a qualitative change of state that can only occur through the fully realized process of construction. Ito's long building history and intimate knowledge of construction mean that he is not bound by the normative dictates of materials use—that concrete should be heavy and sculptural, for example. In his hands, inert matter is transformed into something resembling living matter, and allows his architecture to be light "like a bird, and not like a feather," to borrow Paul Valéry's formulation.[19]

The resemblance of the Berkeley project to a house of cards is highly suggestive. A house of cards is elemental and repeatable—the product of simple operations of balance and stacking, carried out with a given set of standardized parts—at the same time as it is fragile and provisional. To make a house of cards stable, you could add additional elements like glue and tape or manipulate the elements themselves by tearing, bending, or folding them. Ito has done the latter, exercising the minimum necessary morphological transformation in order to impart stability to this fragile assemblage. Far from the conventional image of the art museum as "culture bunker," Ito's museum appears at once as an arrangement of forms caught at an instant of momentary equilibrium and as something inevitable: a recognizable icon assembled from conventional elements.

Language without affect is a dead language: and affect without language is uncommunicable.

—André Green

Ito's work emerged during the 1970s in the midst of architecture's linguistic turn. Yet a simple return to language has never been part of the architect's agenda. For Ito it is the *impossibility* of language—of architecture ever approaching the discursive transparency of written or verbal language—that animates his work. A comparison with the work of two of his peers proves instructive. Arata Isosaki (born in 1931, ten years earlier than Ito) embraced interdisciplinarity, linguistic reference, and, in some projects, overt historical quotation, almost from the beginning of his career. Even when it is not explicitly referential, his work is a collage of ready-made signs. The work of Tadao Ando (Ito's exact contemporary) is, by contrast, resolutely anti-scenographic, emptying architecture of all possible

reference other than light, material, and space. Starting from scratch, he restrains architecture's representational capacity through a heroic act of invention. Ito falls somewhere in between Ando and Isosaki: he is skeptical of both, yet draws productively from each. Although his buildings are richly suggestive and syntactically complex, he never fully engages the linguistic. Legible semantic reference is always kept at a distance: for Ito, that would be too easy, too conciliatory. On the other hand, he is not tempted by the portentous "silence" of Ando, which monumentalizes the impossibility of communication. Ando wants to shut down the referential in order to get at a deeper level of meaning—a non-discursive, phenomenological fullness. Ito is critical of this, recognizing its power (as in the White U) but understanding that a deep level of personal meaning cannot have a wider significance in the public realm. For Ito, such fullness of presence is a given property of architectural experience more than a material with which the architect might work. If Isosaki works with "language without affect" (what he communicates risks topicality and trivialization), Ando works with "affect without language." He risks simply not communicating. Ito's work is delicately poised between affect *and* language: syntactically dense, it is full of meaning and suggestion without ever devolving into literal quotation.

Ito's White U, for example, oscillates between the collective memory of architecture's formal types—a symmetrical courtyard and an apsidal space—and a frank confrontation with the fragility of life in the Post-Nuclear Age. It is this dual engagement that transforms the house into a collective statement beyond the narrative of personal loss. At the Tama Art Library, it is impossible not to read the arches as a sign, a reference to a recognizable form in the repertory of classical architecture. They *are* that, but they are many other things, too: a subtle strategy for partitioning space while enabling visual transparency, an unexpected material transformation, and a knowing echo of the library's collective space. Surely Ito's primary intention was not to make reference to Western classical architecture, but by accepting this reference and its associated meanings—while pursuing innovative structural and spatial solutions and reworking the library's program—Ito produces work that is richer and more nuanced precisely for its capacity to hold these multiple readings in a delicate equilibrium.

It is this suspension—between memory and forgetting, between possibility and impossibility, between language and silence—that makes Ito's work significant today. His skeptical intelligence and restless creativity tell him that the old solutions will no longer work. Yet architecture for him is by no means an exhausted practice. He holds fast to an optimistic idea: that through a patient and slow search, there may be moments, widely spaced and hard-won, when something new emerges. But Ito is not naive. His search is not for a heroic, revolutionary breakthrough but for a fissure, a toehold that will help to move the discipline not so much forward as sideways, or back on itself, revisiting known territory from a new perspective. And that is all architecture can ever do in the present.

NOTES

First Epigraph. Robin Evans, "Figures, Doors and Passages" (1978), reprinted in his Translations from Drawing to Building and Other Essays (London: Architectural Association, 1996), 56.

Second Epigraph. Toyo Ito, cited by Mutsuro Sasaki, in "A Dialogue with Toyo Ito," Morphogenesis of Flux Structure, trans. Thomas Daniell (London: AA Publications, 2007), 62.

1. Le Corbusier, Creation Is a Patient Search, trans. James Palmes (New York: Praeger, 1960).

2. "The 'body of electronic modernism' calls for a still more non-localized space than the one created by mechanistic modernism." Toyo Ito: Blurring Architecture, 1971–2005, ed. Ulrich Schneider and Marc Feustel (Milan: Charta, 1999), 55.

3. See Yve-Alain Bois, "A Picturesque Stroll around Clara-Clara," October 29 (Summer 1984): 32–62, for a description of the perceptual effects of Richard Serra's sculpture on the spectator in motion.

4. Reyner Banham, "A Home Is Not a House," Art in America 2 (April 1965): 109–18;

Toyo Ito, "Dismantling and Reconstituting the 'House' in a Disordered City," in Tarzans in the Media Forest and Other Essays, trans. and ed. Thomas Daniell (London: AA Publications, 2010), 69–71.

5. Toyo Ito, cited in Tatsuo Kuwahara, "Drawing," in Toyo Ito: Blurring Architecture, 105.

6. Alain Robbe-Grillet, "From Realism to Reality," in his For a New Novel: Essays on Fiction, trans. Richard Howard (New York: Grove Press, 1965), 165.

7. Evans, "Figures, Doors and Passages," 55–91.

8. Toyo Ito, cited in Nobuhiro Tsukada, "Reproduction," in Toyo Ito: Blurring Architecture, 83.

9. "The house should be mute on the outside and reveal all of its riches on the interior." Adolf Loos, "Heimatkunst" (1914), in Franz Glück, ed., Adolf Loos: Sämtliche Schriften in zwei Bänden, vol. 1 (Vienna: Herold, 1962), 339; cited by Johan van de Beek in "Adolf Loos: Patterns of Townhouses," in Raumplan versus Plan Libre: Adolf Loos/Le Corbusier, ed. Max Risselada (Rotterdam: 010 Publishers, 2008), 193, n. 5.

10. See Beatriz Colomina, Privacy and Publicity: Modern Architecture as Mass Media (Cambridge, MA: MIT Press, 1996).

11. Ito, cited in Tsukada, "Reproduction," 80.

12. Cited in ibid., 81.

13. Adolf Loos, "Architecture" (1910), in Architecture and Design, 1890–1939: An International Anthology of Original Articles, ed. Tim Benton and Charlotte Benton, with Dennis Sharp (London and New York: Granada, 1980), 45.

14. Ibid.

15. Sasaki, "A Dialogue with Toyo Ito," 55.

16. The full citation reads: "Cinema proceeds with photogrammes—that is, with immobile sections—twenty-four images per second (or eighteen at the outset). But it has often been noted that what it gives us is not the photogramme.... [C]inema does not give us an image to which movement is added, it immediately gives us a movement-image." Gilles Deleuze, Cinema 1: The Movement-Image, trans. H. Tomlinson and B. Habberjam (Minneapolis: University of Minnesota Press, 1986), 2.

17. "Then we have computer science. It is true that software cannot exercise its powers of lightness except through the weight of hardware....The second industrial revolution, unlike the first, does not present us with such crushing images as rolling mills and molten steel, but with 'bits' in a flow of information traveling along circuits in the form of electronic impulses. The iron machines still exist, but they obey the orders of weightless bits." Italo Calvino, "Lightness," in his Six Memos for the Next Millennium (Cambridge, MA: Harvard University Press, 1988), 8.

18. Ironically, Ito's Mediatheque would seem to owe something to another unbuilt OMA project, the 1989 Trés Grande Bibliothèque in Paris. Conceived as a solid block of information, OMA hollowed out spaces of public occupation from the project's cubic volume. Koolhaas and Ito are very different architects: what is interesting here is to see the two distinct architectural responses to a similar organizational or programmatic proposition.

19. Paul Valéry, cited in Calvino, Six Memos for the Next Millennium, 16.

LIQUID SPACE

INTRODUCTION

STAN ALLEN

It is my great pleasure to introduce Toyo Ito, who will give the Kenneth Kassler lecture for 2009.

It seems especially fitting that we turn to such an important architect as Toyo Ito for our endowed lecture this spring. It's also timely, because our students recently traveled to Tokyo to attend a conference that looked at the continuing influence of the Metabolists. Ito has a very direct connection to that generation, having begun working in the office of Kiyonori Kikutake in the 1960s. In 1971, he started his own office in Tokyo, building upon the research and insights of the previous generation. It also seems significant to me that the original name of his studio was Urbot, or Urban Robot, reflecting the concerns of that decade and the influence of the Metabolists. In 1979, the name of the studio was changed to Toyo Ito and Associates.

Parallel to his career as an architect, Ito has taught extensively, as a visiting professor at the University of Tokyo and at Columbia University, where I first met him, in the early 1990s. He's done additional teaching as a visiting professor at UCLA, Kyoto University, and the Tama Art University.

When you start talking about Ito's career and work, the inevitable starting point is the extraordinary White U house, finished in 1976—a house that, although demolished, still to this day has a powerful, hauntingly poetic presence that emerges in the photographs and drawings. Ito was also one of the first architects to think deeply about the implications of digital technologies for architecture and the city. For Ito, the fluidity of twentieth-century subjectivities calls for a different way of being in the city—what he has called the "body of electronic modernism," exemplified in his 1986 project for the Tower of Winds in Tokyo.

What I find extraordinary about Ito's work is his capacity to continually reinvent himself and his practice, without ever losing sight of his core concerns. Around the turn of the twenty-first century, his preoccupation with the architectural consequences of digital technology culminated in his competition-winning project for the Sendai Mediatheque. The building was completed in 2000, and it has become a definitive statement about a certain relationship between organization and information, and the creation of a fluid architectural space that seems to belong uniquely to our time.

It's the mark of any creative intelligence that it continues to innovate, and I think that 2002 signaled another bold new direction in Ito's work with his pavilion for the Serpentine Gallery. The project continues an innovative series of collaborations with structural engineers— Mutsuro Sasaki in the case of the Mediatheque, and Cecil Balmond in the case of the Serpentine. Here, structure and innovation at the level of structural design and its relationship to space become thematic— a line of inquiry that continues to unfold today. This approach, which develops a refinement and clarification and minimization of structure while at the same time exploiting its expressive potentials, is very much in evidence in his recent work: the Tod's Omotesando building completed in 2004, the Tama Art University Library of 2007, and the Taichung Metropolitan Opera House, which is currently under construction.

His first major project in the United States—a project that I am particularly interested in seeing today—is an art museum for the University of California at Berkeley. With its delicate use of structure and space, the Berkeley project almost looks like a house of cards, yet it produces astonishing new spatial effects and brings the diagrammatic to a new level.

Each year the School of Architecture invites an architect of the highest international distinction to deliver our most prestigious lecture, the Kenneth Kassler Lecture. The series was endowed in honor of Kenneth Kassler after his death in 1964. Kassler was a member of the Princeton Class of 1927, and received his MFA here in 1930. He was an instructor at the School from 1930 to 1933, and Chairman of the School's Advisory Council.

The inaugural Kenneth Kassler Lecture was given in 1966 by R. Buckminster Fuller; since then, lecturers have included Peter Eisenman, Arata Isozaki, John Hejduk, Kisho Kurokawa, Reyner Banham, and Kazuyo Sejima. Since 2004, Steven Holl, Rem Koolhaas, Denise Scott Brown, Paulo Mendes da Rocha, and Rafael Moneo have been among those who have delivered the Kassler lecture. It is my great pleasure to welcome Toyo Ito into this distinguished company.

—Princeton University School of Architecture
   April 15, 2009

GENERATIVE ORDER 2009

TOYO ITO

SIMULTANEOUSLY TRANSLATED BY
NORIKO TANIGUCHI

The natural world is extremely complicated and variable, and its systems are fluid—it is built on a fluid world. In contrast to this, architecture has always tried to establish a more stable system.

To be very simplistic, one could say that the system of the grid was established in the twentieth century. This system became popular throughout the world, as it allowed a huge amount of architecture to be built in a short period of time.

However, it also made the world's cities homogenous. One might even say that it made the people living and working there homogenous too.

In response to that, over the last ten years, by modifying the grid slightly I have been attempting to find a way of creating relationships that bring buildings closer to their surroundings and environment.

The first project I would like to share with you is a library for Tama Art University on the outskirts of Tokyo, which was completed in 2007. Here, using crisscrossing lines of arches to gently describe curves, we created another kind of grid.

In order to expand the university, we were asked to build a library. This is a new campus. It is a place with lots of undulations, but the buildings have been placed on a grid system without any particular relationship to the topography of the site itself.

Tama Art University campus view

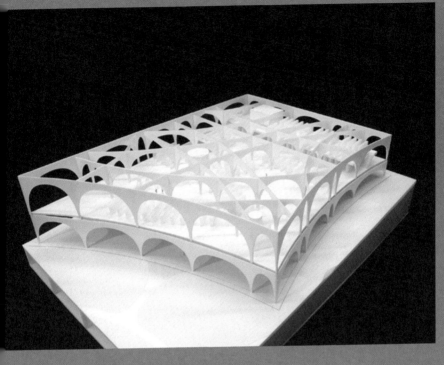

We designed a double-layered building. Again Mr. Sasaki worked with us on the structure, which consists of interlocking arches with spans ranging from roughly six to sixty feet. Almost all of the walls describe a gentle curve in plan.

Model of library structure

Immediately before we began the project, we had been working on this crematorium in rural Japan. The crematorium was not intended to have an accessible roof, but at the opening ceremony I remarked, "Well, the roof is probably the best space in the building," and then everyone started to climb up there. An exception was made, and guests were allowed to explore the roof.

Meiso no Mori Crematorium at Kakamigahara

Roof of the crematorium

The columns of the Tama project were initially conceived for the crematorium. At first we were thinking of using the same kind of columns with curved capitals and a flat roof, but those are really difficult to construct, and also to represent in model. In order to represent the columns in model, we abstracted them as cross shapes describing the outline; this became the form of the arch.

Interior of the crematorium

Formwork for a column

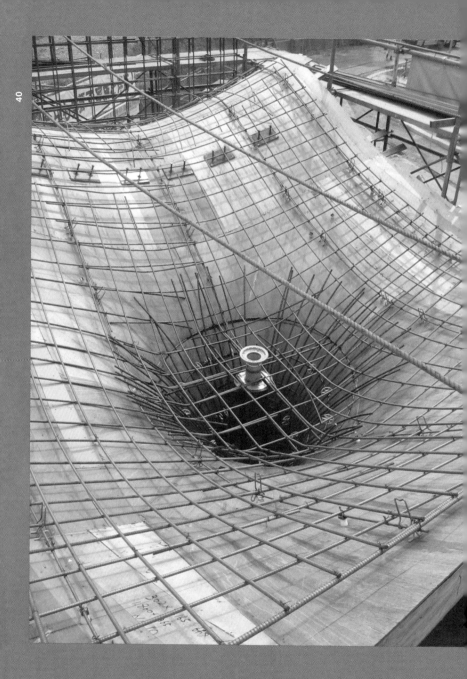

Reinforcement bars for a column

Removing formwork from a cast column

The core of the arch is made of steel, surrounded by reinforcement, with concrete poured on top.

This structural system allowed us not only to make the walls extremely thin but also to create a very small footprint for the column, with the intention that the arch would appear to be floating in space.

Column construction for Tama Art University Library

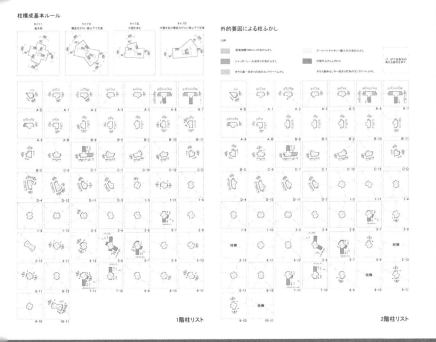

柱構成基本ルール

外的要因による柱ふかし

1階柱リスト

2階柱リスト

We made a diagram that shows the footprints of all of the columns, and as you can see, each one is a different shape.

Diagram of column footprints

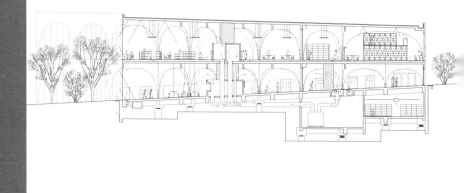

Another characteristic of this building is that, on the first level, the floor has a slope. The surrounding site has a gradient of 1:20, so logically we took that slope and brought it into the building.

On the second level, the floor is flat, but the roof is slightly sloped in the opposite direction.

Section through public route

The lower half of the first floor is a "free space" with a coffee shop, where students can move without restriction. The upper half of the plan is the library itself, which is entered in the center of this drawing.

Most of the floor here is sloped, and the current periodicals counter, the reading area, and the digital media viewing stations are situated here.

Site plan

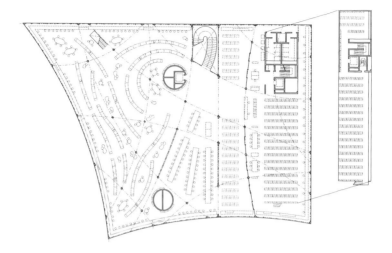

On the second level, most of the space is dedicated to open stacks. The bookshelves gently stitch together the space between the arches. Wrapped around the edge of the building is a counter where students can sit and read, or gaze outside.

The closed-stack area is separated from the open stacks only by a low, glass partition. Students can also study within this area.

Second-floor plan

You can see here how thin the walls of the arches are in this exterior view.

Library exterior

Curved exterior wall

The facade follows a gentle curve. The glass itself also forms a slightly curved surface.

Upper-level interior

Upper-level interior panorama

An open area on the second floor can be used for small
lectures or as a gallery space. On the right-hand side
is the DVD viewing corner. The interesting thing that
I'd like to point out is that although the floor is sloped,
the counter is level. We adjusted the height of the
stools according to the floor in each particular area. We
selected this chair from Germany, the height of which
can be easily adjusted.

Second-floor DVD viewing area

In contrast, the magazine counter follows the slope of the floor—it's pretty uncomfortable to watch a tilted DVD.

The material finishes used in the building are extremely austere. We used minimal finishes on top of the structure.

Second-floor magazine counter

The second project I'd like to discuss is an opera house project in Taichung, Taiwan, which is in planning right now.*

The external form of the building is orthogonal, but the interior is punctured with countless holes, so that levels are connected horizontally and vertically. Cave-like holes penetrate the form.

*Editor's note: This project received approval in November 2009; completion is expected in 2013.

Taichung Metropolitan Opera House entry facade

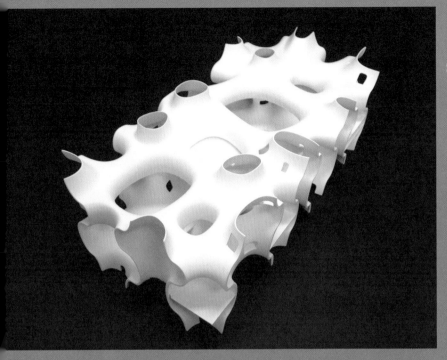

The building will hold three different theaters: one with
two thousand seats, one with eight hundred seats, and
one with two hundred seats. Two large openings in this
model indicate the location of the stage areas for the
two larger theaters.

We are planning to use concrete, and we are collaborat-
ing with Cecil Balmond and his team in London to realize
this complicated structure.

Interior structure of continuous shell

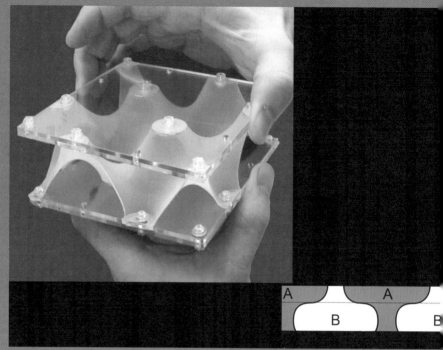

The initial idea for the project came from taking two flat surfaces, dividing them into a grid, and then systematically connecting circles around alternate points vertically with a flexible fabric to create a three-dimensionally curved, continuous surface. If you repeat this form vertically, you get this A/B organization of space, connected vertically and horizontally.

Conceptual model and diagram

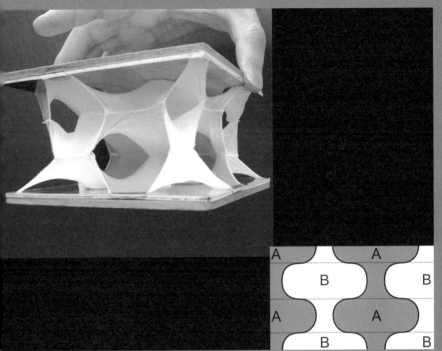

In the vertical direction, the building is made of four levels. By repeating the polyhedrons and then connecting them vertically—and then smoothing them out—we created this structural system.

Double-layered conceptual model and diagram

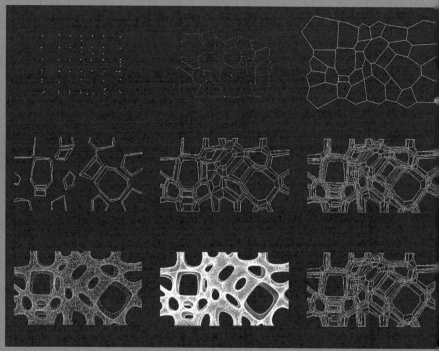

Stills from generative algorithm animation

The interior is a cave-like white space spreading in every direction.

In some areas we submerged the structure to create horizontal floor areas. Depending on the height at which you place the floor, the view of the interior changes considerably.

Interior view of public space

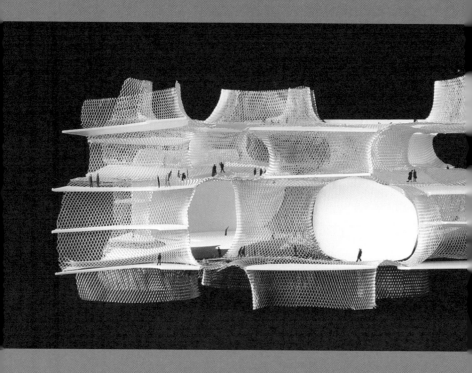

Model, section view

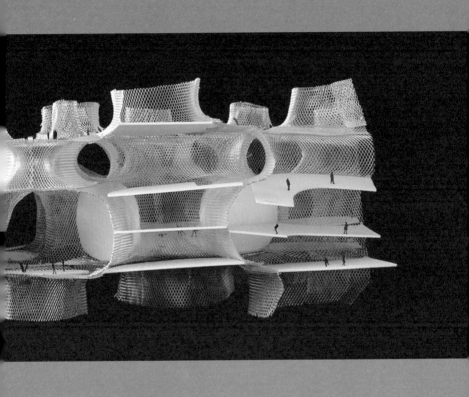

Because the whole of the interior space is made up of continuous convex surfaces, the acoustic quality is very high—much higher than something like a dome.

1:10 acoustic model

The Playhouse is a midsize theater where opera and classical Chinese opera performances will be held.

Eight hundred–seat playhouse

Rooftop garden

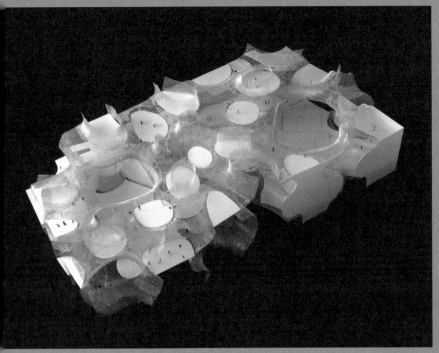

To build our design, we first divided the structure into fifty-six pieces. If you were to take one of those pieces and expand it, you could see that it is a continuous surface made of a series of curved vertical trusses.

Model

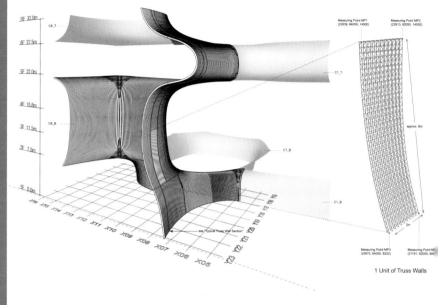

The truss is repeated at twenty-centimeter [eight-inch] intervals. Each truss is a two-dimensional curve, and across the surface, little by little, the form changes to create the three-dimensionally curving surface.

The trusses are connected horizontally, mesh is attached to both sides, and concrete is poured over the surface.

Individual vertical truss within continuous surface

We made a full-scale mockup of one part of the project in Taiwan. I think you can see traces of the mesh on the surface of the concrete. The surface of the actual building will be sprayed or hand-finished in plaster. Almost all of the walls can be made at a thickness of forty centimeters [sixteen inches].

Full-scale structural mockup of one of the fifty-six pieces

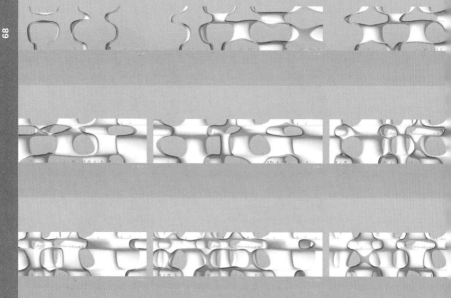

These sections are cut at ten-centimeter [four-inch] intervals and then connected. If you were to take a horizontal planometric cut, the effect would be almost the same.

At this point, all of the design is complete. We're just waiting for a construction company to take on the job. If somebody will take it on, construction can start right away.

Series of stills from sectional animation

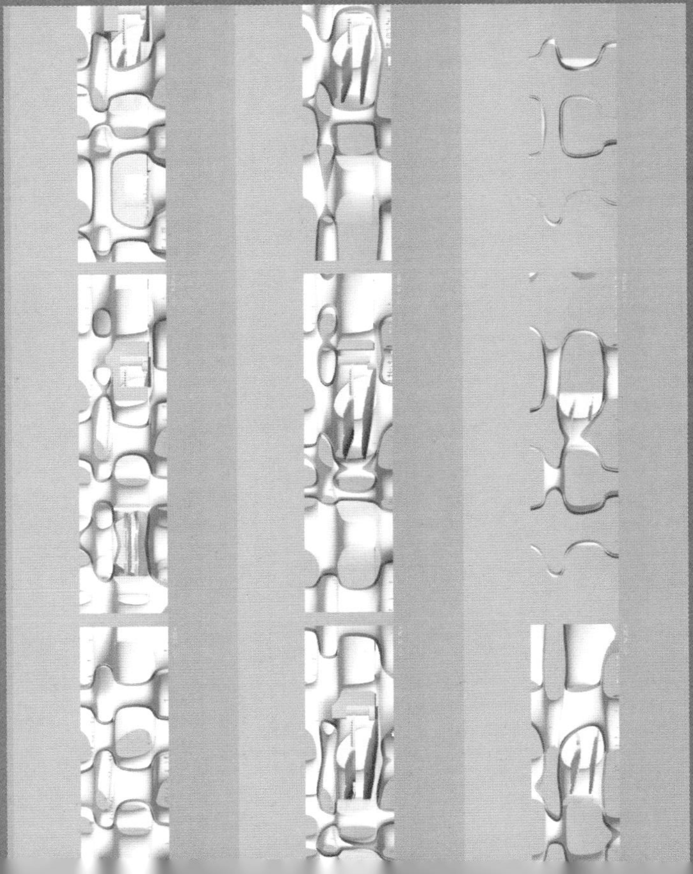

Existing BAM/PFA

New Site

The last project I'd like to introduce is the University of California Berkeley Art Museum and Pacific Film Archive [BAM/PFA] complex, which is just approaching the peak of the design development phase.

The site for this project is extremely exciting: it faces the main gate of the campus. Moreover, it is backed by the grid of the city.

The BAM/PFA buildings currently exist on this site, but they sustained considerable damage in the San Francisco earthquake of 1989, and while they have been repaired and are in use, it was decided to rebuild them.

Berkeley Art Museum and Pacific Film Archive site view

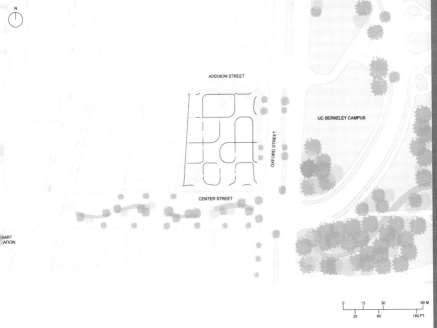

ADDISON STREET

OXFORD STREET

UC BERKELEY CAMPUS

CENTER STREET

BART
STATION

N

0   15   30   60 M
     30   90   180 FT

While following the grid of the city, I also wanted to superimpose the fluid green space of the campus.

Ordinarily professors and students use this site, but the people of the city use it simultaneously, and so it has become a kind of nodal point.

BAM/PFA site plan

A midscale project, the building has three stories above ground and a total floor area of 135,000 square feet. The structure has one peculiar characteristic: we are using a structural system consisting of concrete sandwiched between two steel plates, which is currently undergoing fire testing.

Main entrance facade facing Center Street

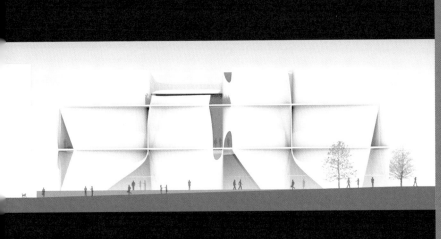

We are working with the engineer Mutsuro Sasaki,
whom we had worked with on the Sendai Mediatheque.
The walls are extremely thin. In all likelihood, we will
be able to make the walls throughout the building only
12.7 centimeters [5 inches] thick.

Longitudinal section showing public route through building

ADDISON STREET

OXFORD STREET

CENTER STREET

N

1F plan

1 Main Entrance
2 Sub Entrance
3 Office & Academic Entrance
4 Black Box Space
5 Gallery
6 Public Gallery
7 MATRIX Gallery
8 Collection Gallery
9 Special Exhibition Gallery
10 Works on Paper Gallery
11 Asian Collection Gallery

12 Gallery EV Lobby
13 Restaurant
14 Kitchen
15 Retail
16 Theater Lobby & Gallery
17 Theater
18 Loading Dock
19 Children's Studio
20 Art & Film Library
21 PFA Library Storage
22 Screening Room

23 Works on Paper Study Center
24 Print & Drawing Study Center
25 Asian Art Study Center
26 Learning Center
27 Seminar Room
28 Vista Space
29 Office
30 Event Space
31 Terrace
32 Asian Garden

0   10   20   30 m
10   30   60   90 ft.

First-floor plan

Galleries flank the Center Street entrance on the first floor. Passing through the foyer of the theater, you connect to the other entrance.

A retail area and a cafe with about eighty seats are located near the entrance, facing Center Street.

Main entrance view

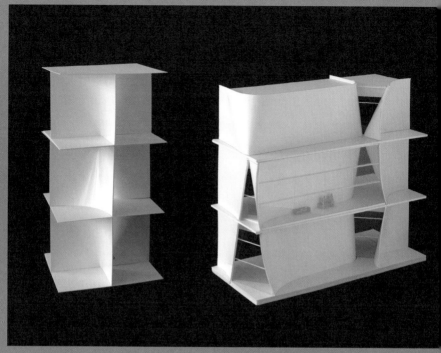

A museum ordinarily has a lot of wall space, but rather than cut holes in the walls to create openings, I wanted to bend the walls and have the visitors slip or slide in between the gaps. I wanted to express the comings and goings of people like water flowing through.

Detail models

Facing Addison Street is a two hundred fifty–seat theater.

Theater interior

3F Asian Collection Gallery and Gar
Asian Art Study Center
Event Space
Office
Terrace

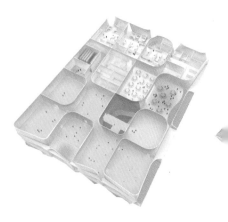

Art galleries are shown in pink. If you would like to view
the exhibition located on the upper floors, you must buy
a ticket before proceeding to Gallery One. Behind that
gallery is the black box, an enclosed area where media
projections take place. The space can also be used as
another theater.

Layout axonometric

2F
Collection Gallery
Special Exhibition Gallery
Works on Paper Gallery
Learning Center
Works on Paper Study Center
Print & Drawing Study Center
Library
Screening Room

1F
Main Entrance
Public Gallery
MATRIX Gallery
Gallery
Black Box Space
Theater
Restaurant
Retail

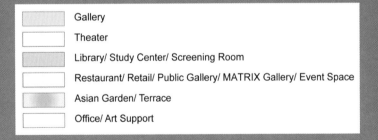

- Gallery
- Theater
- Library/ Study Center/ Screening Room
- Restaurant/ Retail/ Public Gallery/ MATRIX Gallery/ Event Space
- Asian Garden/ Terrace
- Office/ Art Support

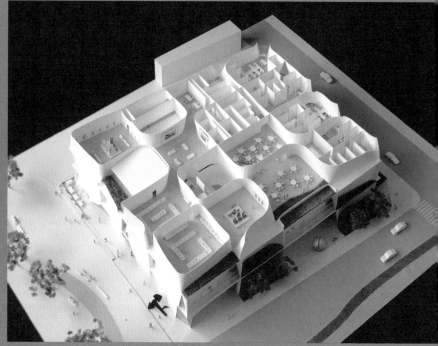

Using the stairs or the elevator, you proceed up to the next level. When you reach the second floor, you have nine gallery spaces: four are for the permanent collections, four house special exhibitions, and the final gallery is for the exhibition of smaller works on paper.

In addition, there are art study centers on the west side of the building; in the northeast corner will be the film archive and its library.

Model

On the third floor, there are seven spaces dedicated to the Asian collection. There is also an event space, where receptions can be held, adjacent to the terrace that over-looks the campus.

Third-floor Asian collection gallery

Separating

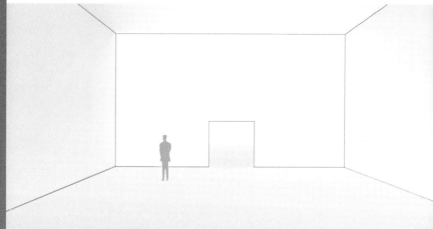

Normally, in the so-called white cube gallery spaces,
you move through holes opened in walls that divide one
space from its neighboring space.

Normal grid

Merging

In contrast to that, we took the bottom of the corner area and, using a curve, opened it, or moved it away. We used the curve to open the top corner and create visual relationships. We used this system in both the horizontal and the vertical dimension to create continuity.

Merged grid

It would be awesome if the walls themselves could
actually move.

Series of stills from concept animation

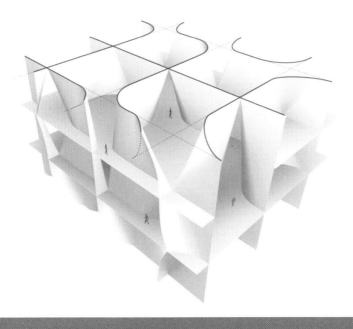

Through this kind of operation, the interior wall becomes the exterior wall, or the exterior turns into the interior. Through the repetition of this inversion you create a relationship between gallery spaces, as if you are walking along one long ribbon of wall.

Spatial system stacking diagram

In the public gallery, you can just see the green outside through the sub-entrance beyond the theater.

In some places there are corners that cannot be used and are not suitable for exhibiting, so we've used them for entrances.

As it stands now, if everything goes according to plan, construction of the Berkeley Art Museum and Pacific Film Archive should start one year from now.*

*Editor's note: the project was halted in 2010 due to financial constraints.

Model

Detail model

To finish, I'd like to explain the title of my lecture,
"Generative Order." The easiest way to understand it
is to learn from the image of a single tree.

A tree assumes its form depending upon its variety.
By repeating very simple rules, the tree creates a very
complex order.

But a tree also decides its own specific form as it grows.
A tree decides its shape in response to its surroundings.
A tree is always open toward the environment.

When you stand beneath a tree—within the span of its
branches, within the space it creates—it is impossible
to determine whether you are inside or outside.

Generative order as a tree

SOCIAL ECOLOGIES

A FRAMEWORK FOR RELATIONSHIPS WITH THE CITY

JESSIE TURNBULL

Beginning with one of Ito's first built projects, the White U, this essay draws out the ideas that would coalesce to form its neighbor, the Silver Hut (1984). He draws an extended analogy between *sacred* and *profane* spaces, terms that can be understood very roughly as designed and undesigned, or formal and informal. He likens the *sacred* to centralized spaces, which inherently have a more traditional composition, and the *profane* to homogenous spaces, structured by the rational universal grid of modernism. The interaction of the two types of space becomes a way of structuring the relationship between the experience of the interior and the exterior of Ito's architecture.

The pair of terms also operates on the level of the city: through the interaction of these two sets of devices, Ito seeks to bring his architecture into a dialogue with the fabric of the city that it inhabits. The essay predates Ito's well-documented body of work on the ephemeral nature of the city as media but uses many of the same metaphors and analogies, comparing buildings to non-physical entities like novels and images. The White U provides an abstract formal canvas upon which Ito tests his ideas, but also functions as an enduring example of architecture that withstands the changing trajectory of his evolving theories, from the real through the mediated and back to the expressively structural, as discussed in "Toyo Ito's Patient Search" in this book.

The effects that he achieves on a domestic scale with the White U and the Silver Hut can be seen as mirrored—architecturally and urbanistically—in his public projects, such as the Sendai Mediatheque, Tama Art University Library, and Berkeley Art Museum and Pacific Film Archive. Issues of surface and structure, as discussed in his 2009 lecture, emerge in this early writing as concepts, as does Ito's preoccupation with the natural in constant battle with the grid.

THE REFLECTION OF THE SACRED IN THE PROFANE WORLD 1978

TOYO ITO

TRANSLATED BY JESSIE TURNBULL

FIRST PUBLISHED IN JAPANESE IN SHINKENCHIKU MAGAZINE, JUNE 1980

1. From the City

About three years ago, an article about my White U house was published in *Shinkenchiku* magazine.[1] In the accompanying photograph, you can just make out the landscape of Tokyo, with its utility poles and the tiled roofs of traditional Japanese *minka* houses. Tracing an arc like the bowl of an earthenware mortar, the concrete structure in the foreground gives a completely different impression than the scenery in the distance. The contrast between the space of a small, artificial universe and the surrounding, anonymous city is striking. The image caption reads as follows: "This house, as you look at it, is a vision. It is as if it has been buried underground. It is so closed. As I thought that, I wondered if the dimly white interior was really 'white.' That is the concept of darkness."[2]

The article's author, Koji Taki, describes the house as a ceramic bowl, but in fact the surface of its roof, which traces an arc and creates the focus of the house, is designed to converge upon a single point, converging like the surface of an inverted cone. At the time of its design, the White U was thought of as simply a study in the manipulation of functional form. But the complementary spatial relationship within this house, like those of the pyramids and cave dwellings—things rightfully called "primordial houses," with strong symbolic form—brings forth some kind of meaning. If the mountain, for example, simultaneously symbolizes the sky, then similarly, if you take the cone as the positive, the space becomes the negative form. In this way the idea of "darkness," and of the house as "buried" underground, becomes something with which I can wholeheartedly agree. Another architect described this house as "symbolic of void."[3] It might seem like a dangerous translation into words of a direct reaction to the space, but thinking about it now, it is a rather skillful description of the space's character.

In reality, the two opposing natures of this house can be analyzed along the lines of André Leroi-Gourhan's peripatetic space on the inside and the radial space in the enclosed courtyard garden, with the centripetal force of the main living section erased and the constant force of the center's periphery circling around and around. But it would be inaccurate to say that this peripatetic movement has no centrifugal force.

Achieved almost without consciousness, the latent originality of this spatial inclination, which the photographs of the space and the criticism make apparent, came as a great shock to me as the designer. In the case of the White U, I had honestly not analyzed it that closely. The strong contrast that these two worlds suggest is far beyond what I had imagined: on the far side, the endlessly extending space of the city, and on the near side, within the form of the house, an air-pocket-like singularity. From the interior, when even that glimpse of cityscape disappears, the White U becomes completely dark. For architects, the space of shadow has a particular, mysterious charm: upon entering, architects fall, as if sliding into a doodlebug's pit, and the logical connection to this world, or even the logical connection to this epoch's sensibility, might be lost entirely.[4]

I have not been able to get this photograph out of my head since then. How can one, in reality, reopen this closed space to the city? How can one coherently re-link to the city? I have been thinking about how to recover context. The reason I keep saying I want to make lightweight architecture is out of concern for this point. And at last, just recently, I have begun to think of ways in which I can open up my own architecture to the city. This is a result of broadening architectural space to include experimentation with spatial concepts that were developed by several architects and critics in the late 1970s, a time when the cultural discourse was invigorated and architecture was resituated within the realm of the city.[5] All sorts of deeply interesting problems have arisen that have to do with the techniques for creating architecture that would not normally have appeared if structure remained limited: one by one, words like *surface*, *vagueness*, *duplicity*, *discrepancy*, and *ambiguity* took architecture from inside its closed genre and lifted it up and threw it into a wider cultural domain; by the time it was thrown back, it had acquired a new meaning: it had recovered the incentive of animated space.

In addition to overcoming modern architecture's reputation for being dissociated with its social context, this kind of movement served to expose its real character and call it into question. The complete situation is, as always, chaotic, but the end result is that the intellectual experiments of the period influenced one another enough to produce some sort of speculative condition; this process of trial and error gradually brought forth the sculptural relief of modern architecture, while breaking down the seemingly established tenets of the Enlightenment. This shifting situation has settled into the opposition of the words *modern* and *postmodern*, but the problem that becomes apparent is that there is an overlap in cultural condition between the two terms.

Accordingly, the two different spaces shown in this one photograph, having raised the issue of the order of space within this expanded cultural and intellectual field, then ask, *How does architectural space open up to the city, and in addition, by what method does the space accomplish that?* These are the questions upon which I would like to muse.

2. Sacred–Profane

The view from the rooftop of the White U is much like the view of any other residential district in a Japanese city. The mid-rise collective housing and the high-rises of the neighboring Shinjuku business district slide into view. The common assumption is that a homogeneous frame of modern buildings organizes the city of Tokyo, and this indeed forms one aspect of the city. But the city also consists of disordered, naturally emerging buildings. Modern architecture infringes on the territory of this other architecture, and as it ushers the city's fabric toward a systematic ordering, this continual struggle gives the city a mysterious vitality.

These two competing territories are, in reality, what make up the city. At first glance this suggests contrasting spaces, but if you take as a starting point, for example, Mircea Eliade's description of space (that is, space which is divided into two opposing varieties—space that is *sacred* and space that is *secular,* or *profane*), one could say that the city belongs to the latter.[6] Of course, Eliade's definitions of *sacred* and *profane* are rooted in a philosophical perspective, but these terms may also be applied to physical space. Modern architecture's universal space has characteristics of homogeneity and relativity, and can therefore be considered part of the *profane* world. But the space of naturally emergent architecture is chaotic and disorderly, and also exhibits mundane qualities that are associated with the *profane* world. In short, whether it is modern architecture or informal development, in cities we live surrounded by *profane* space.

Our bodily experience of the city develops following various undulations. For example, if you were to walk down a bustling street, your attention would be concentrated on continuous, unmediated, fascinating spaces. Walking through Tokyo, the storefronts buried in gaudy accessories piled one on top of the other, left, right, and center, we are completely surrounded by a thin veil of extreme color and ornament. In a European city, you would not find the same extreme experience: there is no other place where the glittering veil covers space so completely that it becomes part of our attire. This experience envelops our bodies completely.

But if we were to tear away this thin veil of fascinating bodily experience, the only thing left would be the homogeneous framework of the space. The modern man, an atheist human, negates the *sacred* world, and lives solely in this framework of flat, undifferentiated space. Eliade writes, "The 'world' already ceased to exist, all things have disintegrated into dust and become fragments of the universe, the industrial society in which man was pursued around and around by his obligations, innumerable, is no more than a cluster of more-or-less neutral 'places' of non-fixed form."[7]

Modern man is completely immersed in this kind of flat space, which we will call *profane* space. Where, in contrast, does *sacred* space exist? According to Eliade, "In the middle of an endless homogeneous space without landmarks, nothing to give any bearings, one absolute *fixed point*, one *center*, is enveloped by holy reincarnation." This is a world where ontology is born. In short, this is a universe based on a premodern understanding of the world, the situating of space in a fixed place.[8] If we were to think of the White U in terms of *sacred* and *profane* space, we would find centrifugal rather than homogeneous space, order rather than disorder, the word universe as opposed to chaos: this is the type of space with which we are dealing. Rather than a discussion of functionality, there is a discussion of abstraction. Rather than a world of relativity, there is a world of ontology.

Modern architecture, no matter what heroic pose it strikes, has as the basis of its model homogeneity, relativity, and universality, and comes from the aesthetics of *profane* space.

But in reality, the resulting spaces don't necessarily conform to the model. They don't conform to the model because they are evaluated within the architectural context of modernism.

For example, if we look at Le Corbusier, who was at the center of the modern movement, his works that bore the most criticism were his later ones, like the monastery of La Tourette and the chapel at Ronchamp. Indicated in those spaces is the form of an architect who desired darkness and was surrounded by nature. Or take the spaces with which Louis Kahn charmed everyone in the 1960s: the centrality excluded by modernist tenets can be clearly read in these spaces. Within works that are read as modern, there are many, like these, that possess a strong centrality and that create a closed universe. This demonstrates that even modern architects long for the *sacred* space that violates the modernist model. Ever since Walter Benjamin pointed out the loss of aura in the 1920s,other fine arts genres have denied this reduction of authenticity. But even as we understand that we inhabit the *profane* world, we—and architects especially—are somehow, in some sense, always attached to this *sacred* space.[9]

This kind of longing by architects for *sacred* space is based on the myth of *the house as model of the world*, and architects are, of course, the hands that build that *house*, that *model*. If the roof or dome that forms the *house* symbolizes heaven, the supports that hold up the roof connect heaven and earth, and represent the center of the world. Accordingly, this myth of the world shows that the action of making a house creates order out of chaos and gives structure, form, and norms by which to shape the universe.

From the moment of its formation, modern architecture exhaustively discarded the concept of *house as model of the world*. In order to rid the word *house* of historical connotations there was an attempt to eliminate the icon of the *house* and replace it with the clean *vessel*. This is true iconoclasm. But it is not so simple to, through a change in ideology, abstract a concept that has for so long been central to the thought of our world. Even if we don't use the specific words "central to our world," when one talks about *space* with even a little feeling, for architects the word *house* is already implied, and the concept of the universe has already entered the conversation. Even when it is simply a matter of pragmatic problem solving, we have a strong desire to give space a center, to give it a conclusive order. Every architect has had the experience at an everyday level of design of simply setting one axis line or one central point, and, like a knitting unraveling, planning is set in motion, and almost automatically order emerges based on that axis or point. This line or point holds such allure that it is difficult to break away from its persuasive power. This is just one technical aspect of design but, when related to the configuration of architecture, the dynamics of the centralized space are so hard to resist that you subconsciously submit to them. Charles Jencks estimates that, in most countries, neoclassicism comes around every twenty-five years, but from the repetition of this type of architecture created from these most original architectural elements we can also ask, *Do people have a particular proclivity toward centrality and axiality*?

If these two spaces of the *sacred* and the *profane* really do exist, for we who live in the world of the *profane*, even if today's *sacred* spaces carry an elevated meaning, could they be *commonly owned* by the people living within the city, if we don't hide these spaces but rather apprehend them as architecture? This is what I'd like to discuss here. No matter how much people would like to hide their longing for *sacred* space, the present we are living in is a homogeneous world divided by function into its constituent parts. Even though the abstract world existed around us until the recent past, there is no reason to expect that we might reverse that trajectory entirely now. As Eliade writes, "Modern man's *personal religion*—his dreams and desires—is already no more than a myth of ontology. The reason is that it was never shared holistically, and therefore it never changed from an individual to a typical situation."[10] And so, in the first place, elevating this individual situation to a typical situation is extremely difficult, and then, on top of that, we want to add *common ownership* of this space. The only way to achieve this *common ownership* is to open it up toward the city.

3. The Space of the Transition

In today's architectural world, no matter how many words like *after modernism* or *postmodernism* journalists coin, these terms are part of an extremely fixed system and do nothing more than redirect our attention back to modern architecture. That systemization and fixity does not just create clusters of buildings that form anonymous cities filled with homogeneous spaces, but stretches farther, to the perception of the architects themselves. We hear concerns that most architects who make housing today are like the fountains in the middle of shopping malls, garnering popularity by behaving as *vessels* within the territory of safe, harmless modern design. No matter how ingeniously camouflaged this domestic space, beneath its cloak of cheap Western humanism, or exposed concrete, or superficial abstract form, you will easily discover that it is constructed according to a system based on everyday aesthetics. Such is the extent to which, with a fresh spirit of attack, the progressive characteristics of modern architecture continue to win us over and make us conservative.

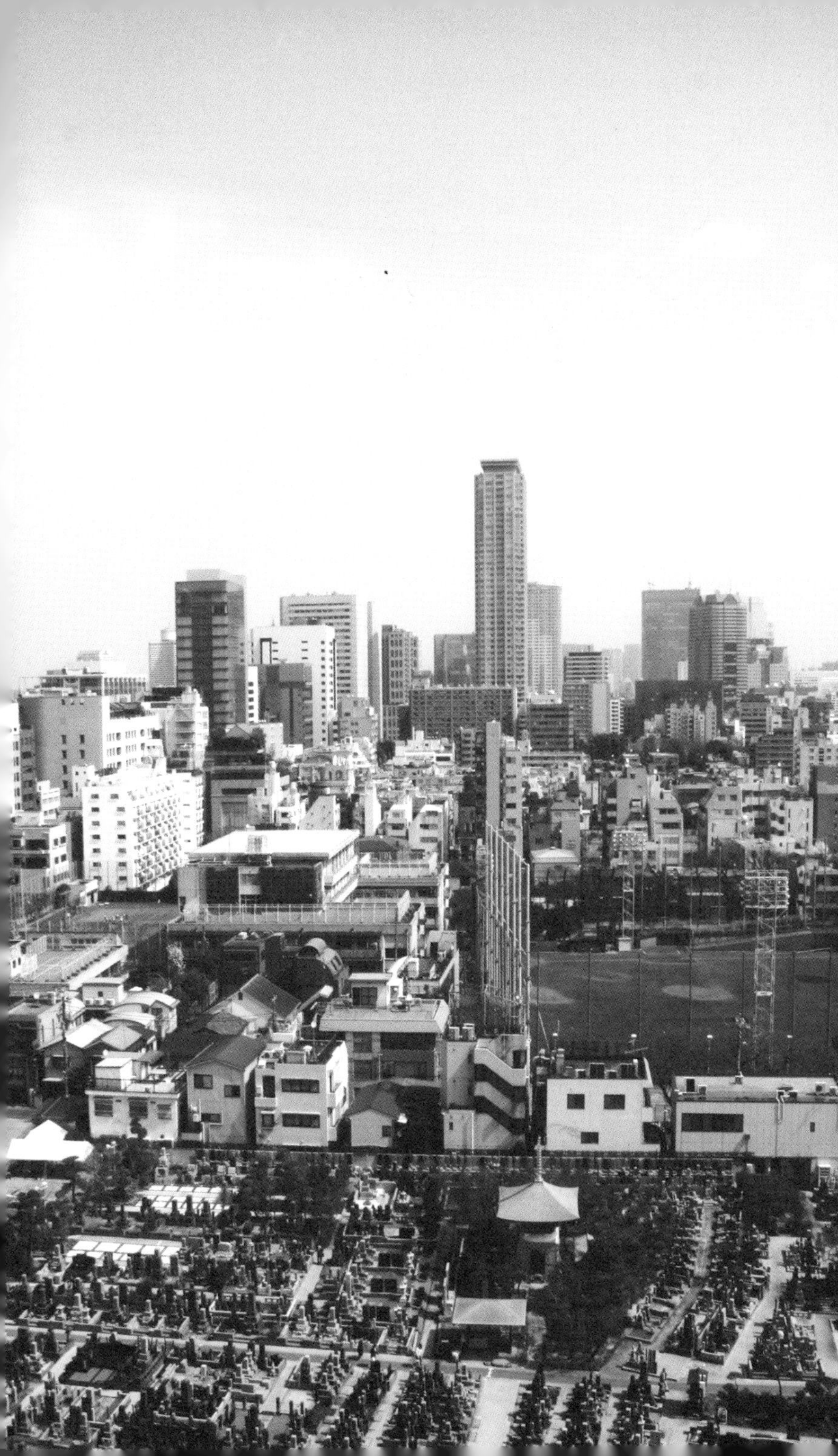

But as much as the territory of this kind of fixed system expands, at the same time, the whirling stress of the urban population, which cannot be contained within the comfort of the *vessel* (and the phenomenon that arises along with it), cannot go unnoticed. Take, for example, the small residential tracts known as mini-developments, which emerge without the taint of that poisonous hobby and touch the landscape at the point where their homogeneous frames hit the ground. Why is there a sense of affinity with this type of building? Or, in a similar vein, the addition of those roofs covered in garish tiles to condominium buildings: what is the meaning of this?

The terrible physical state of the residential territory is indication enough of their inefficiency as housing. But this building stock fulfills the peoples' unchanging desire for a *house*, and in appealing to that desire we evade a system of regulations and continually save energy.

The space of modernism that is turning into conservativism is a kind of *profane* space, but buried within the city the chaos of the naturally occurring housing tracts are creating a new type of *profane* space. Even if we were to call it the same *profane*, the modernist space takes its form by shedding its inextricable links to associations with the *house* through the iconoclasm of architecture, whereas the latter exists within the disorder and is latent in the constant yearning for the universe of the *house*. Can the two understandings of the house ever come into contact? The urban populace yearns for the *house*, in their mundane city lives. But can their latent yearning ever come close to the aforementioned mysticism of the *house* that has taken root and is latent in the emotional depth of the architects who still practice modernism? Or are the two completely different concepts? The modern architect's concept of the *house* can be thought of as a violation of the functionalist tenets of the modernist model, and so the relationship between the house and the tenets is strained. In short, as an emotional counterpart to technique, and as an expression of the beauty of abstraction in opposition to functionality, the *house* emerged from deep within the homogeneity of modernism as a spiritually uplifting antithesis to the *model of the world*. As modernism expressed this homogeneous order as heroic, the architecture of the *house* emerged as an opposing concept: what architects conceive as *sacred* space must also strengthen its heroic characteristics. The peculiarity of this modernist architecture is that it cuts the *profane* world wide open, and it builds an invented everyday space, one that on the other hand we could call religious. In order for this *typicalization* to be realized as a *model*, it had to go through a series of exclusive removals. This positioned the modernist spread of space in opposition to time, against which the robust spirit of architecture must struggle to create *sacred* space.

The world of the *house* becomes isolated as *sacred* space. It has acquired great distance from the *profane house*, which has sunk to the bottom of architectural meaning through the yearning for an icon. And this distance is the distance of the gap between the city and architecture that we first touched upon. Even though people are often struck by the strength of the condensed space of the *world as model*, the *common ownership* of this space is still extremely difficult. In contrast to this, the *profane* world—with its ongoing, latent longing for the *sacred*, and its inability to hold order—descends into chaos, and only that fragment of a phenomenon goes up in flames. This is the world of the city's potential energy that the architect has hitherto neglected.

For the modernists—who are immersed in the *profane* world— the space of architecture is first and foremost a *vessel*, but at the same time it must meet the needs of a *house*. We must turn our attention to the space that results from the desire to recognize the contradiction of something wanting to be both a *vessel* and a *house*. Through this, architects have a way of relating people to the city that they inhabit. And in order to retrieve the *profane* world from the depths of the subconscious—to reinstate sentiments like the *sacred*, and *communal ownership*, that support the space of the city—we create an architecture that is inherently ambiguous. In other words, this is the point where the spaces of the two alien worlds—the *sacred* and the *profane*—become mingled.

Some time ago I wrote an article entitled "One Day the Points of Interplay between Le Corbusier and Venturi Will Create an Architecture."[11] At the time, my thoughts on the work of those two architects weren't necessarily fully developed in my mind, but essentially what I tried to predict was that, in the opposition within architecture of things that are modern and things that are postmodern, complex points of interplay would result in an ambiguous and obscure architecture. It is the kind of space that becomes functional if you think it is abstract; if you think it has centrality, it becomes homogeneous; if it looks extraordinary, it becomes spatially mundane. Venturi was the first architect who showed me that the architecture that modernists believed was the pinnacle of the abstract and *sacred* was in fact subconsciously proliferating throughout the *profane* world.

This way in which the *sacred* mixed with the *profane* is not like a brilliant space glimpsed through a crevice in the *profane* but is rather like the shadow cast on a paper screen, or an ink stain on a piece of *washi* paper: the *sacred* is a world floating ambiguously within the space of the *profane*. One could also say that the *sacred* draws out from the bottom of the stagnant depths of the *profane* world to a height where it becomes clear. However we say it, in this space resulting from the mix of *sacred* and *profane*, there will be a continued spatial interchange from *sacred* to *profane* and conversely, from *profane* to *sacred*. To put it in architectural terms, the continued reciprocal motion in space from the *house* to the *vessel*, from the *vessel* to the *house*, is born from this interaction. In short, the interference of two desires—the desire to order the form of the universe that implies the *house*, and the desire for an everyday, relativist *vessel*—produces discrepancies and mixings, and the dynamics of this activate the spaces within.

This could be misinterpreted, but if you were to try to concretely express the image of this ambiguous space, you could immediately make a living by creating shining examples of small housing tracts. From the point of view of design, there is nothing worse than the poor quality of housing developments, but, as I have already mentioned, in that space there is a vitality that can never be eliminated. This is formed of a completely different vocabulary—and a completely different structure—and in that vocabulary there still exists the glittering desire for the icons of history and territory of which modernism would wish to dispose. These structures, while hiding the desire for iconography, provide a poisonous decoration that becomes integrated with structural elements like doors, windows, and balconies; in this way, quite apart from being unable to understand the structure visually, anyone can digest the form and draw a common image from it. This overlaps with people's preconception of what a *house* should be.

But even if the crude power of disorderly developer housing has always existed, it will remain as such until we examine it as a phenomenon. It is possible to give a brilliance to space by polishing up all the vocabulary that preserves the icon, and recombining that polished vocabulary into a special flexible system that increases the utility of the *container* without losing

any of its vigor. This kind of brilliance is certainly not captured by realism; it is only obtained through its symbolic power, and when that becomes possible, the housing tract comes into cultural value as a house.

Let us also take a look at another concrete image: the homogeneous, functional space created by the structural frame, in the moment that it suddenly begins to dissolve and become unstable. This is like the spreading of an ink stain; for example, because of the inclination within the frame toward the *sacred*, the action of a centralizing force creates a friction with the frame that generates an instantaneous space. Here the mutual movement—from *profane* to *sacred*, and the distortion of the *profane* by the *sacred*—occurs, and through that movement the frame is softly distorted, and the facade begins to shimmer like undulating waves. This mall fountain that seemed so safe and harmless gushes out. After continued melting, the frame essentially disappears, and only a collage of elements colored by the shadow of an icon remains. This architecture is a non-visual structure, and floats like a heat haze within this homogeneous space.

We often hear that these kinds of physical changes taking place in transitional conditions are the most unsettling and formidable for human beings. According to Akira Yamaguchi, another way of expressing these changes in form is through the word "mix" (*majiru*), and by replacing the character for *ma* with a different character meaning space or interval, so of course it seems dangerous to humans.[12] The vitality of the mixed space of the *sacred* and *profane* is derived from the sense of danger at the moment of moving from one type of organization to another. This is also the process of incorporating and activating the ambiguous periphery—the boundary between the territories of culture and non-culture.

4. Superficiality/Surface Evolution as Technique

Today, *shared space* lies within the *profane* world in which we are submerged, but if you mix in the *sacred*, a kind of shadow portrait space is formed. This is certainly not the rarified space created by slicing up the world in the linear progression of the parallel sections. If not that, then without a *contrivance* to purify the turbid, opaque deposit of the *profane*, like inserting a glimpse of the *sacred* or viewing the clear outlines of a shadow cast upon the back of a sheet of murkily opaque *washi* paper, this kind of space shouldn't be able to exist. This goes without saying, but what we're calling a *contrivance* here isn't merely a technique of architectural technology. Instead, it could be called the emergence of a means for architecture to create architecture as an intellectual method. *Contrivances* can be used in relation to the novel: "This word contrivance is used to indicate people's range of complete lifestyle change…[and] when thinking about writing techniques, the use of this word contrivance and the work it does"is the same as the word *technique*.[13] For example, if we watch a drama—even if we fall about laughing and weeping, if we become drawn into the storyline—in the background we still have a sense of the construction of its space; similarly, in the space of architecture, the power of symbolism is awakened within the darkness of the subconscious. An architect trying to physically unsettle that balance would need a cool eye to carefully select and unite the vocabulary of the *sacred* and the *profane*.

But a skillful drama or novel conceals the device within the rich description of each scene, and we adduce our measurement of the novel's space through that. Furthermore, the subject of today's dramas and novels are generally centered on everyday, recurring events, so the space that the story opens up is limited to the mundane. As we approach a catastrophe or climax, deep and complex problems concerning love or family are endured with a subtle smile or grimace within an otherwise ordinary expression or exchange, with no dramatic depth of space. Accordingly, a drama or novel that is centered on the everyday isn't without depth; rather, it has a conventional construction, and characters suspended within this superficial ordinariness weave meaningful narratives.

Architecture also creates spaces through a construction of rich surface vocabulary, through which it conceals its devices. And the richness of this skin changes the very nature of the device, eventually becoming enough to erase the substance of the surface and reveal its potential: in the end, surface itself becomes architecture. There is a propensity today to require architectural space to be heavy and substantial, with the capacity to protect, but this architectural space cannot simply be dismissed as surface, or something frivolous and unreliable. This space doesn't lack depth of structure. Through discarding conventional independent structure and achieving structural depth within this apparently superficial architecture, we bring in elements of the *sacred*. In short, the depth of this *sacred* space is compressed into the surface, and the only way to experience depth is for the person to circumnavigate the walls of the space. No depth is revealed through the breaking of this surface.

Today, the surface/depth relationship is not defined by the simple consequence of the opposition of an unreliable phenomenological surface to the decisive existence of depth, but rather it is such that the two are reflexively tied together in a circuit where they simultaneously refer to one another. Because of an impetus toward depth, the structural effect of surface emerges like an electric shock, and in a subconscious moment depth appears as surface. This instantaneous, electric, current-like movement is the *device* that creates a mechanism for flexible feedback, both in novels and in architecture.

After the White U, I came up with several *devices* for turning architecture into an experience. One of these was the technique of *masking* architecture. This concept started with the notion of testing a way to apply the facade as a false *mask* on the exterior, in opposition to the modernist tenet that the volume created by architecture must be directly reflected in its exterior form. In the case of the White U, the facade that faces the road is different from all those adjacent to it, both in materials and in form, emphasizing the character of its outside skin in relation to the homogeneous frame of the interior space. This exterior skinning behaves like a camouflage for the building—the house is hidden within the city—but it is also a technique deployed by commercial architecture that was ignored by modernists. This *device* is encompassed within the undesirable realm of commercial architecture, and is therefore beyond the remit of modernist tenets, rendering the *device* of surface a free genre.

This experiment was succeeded by another, similar one, where the physical construction of the frame's composition became an expression of the discrepancy between structure and external surface. This kind of surface expression is practiced today by many different architects, but the *device* must be more than a visual expression of discrepancy, or it is exposed as simply a manipulation of consciousness and rendered nothing more than a logical development of the original modernist lesson of the Dom-ino House. The discrepancy between surface and interior is not simply a way to recognize the *device* of planned discord between architecture and skin: when the *device* of the *mask* uses the system of discrepancies to change the form (without negating it), suddenly the resultant space becomes activated. Through this, the *mask* and the power that it holds are revealed.

In my recent works, I have become more interested in the general problem of discrepancy between interior and exterior than in the facade specifically. From the exterior, the White U effectively behaves as a *house*: it is constantly carrying out the abstract function of striving for centrality. The interior, on the other hand, is like a machine that fabricates contained space. The real test of this architecture is to reveal the reciprocity of these two opposing activities. There is an interstice created by opposing these two types of space: a space focused on centrality and a space that is purely mechanical. The ambiguity created by this spatial opposition gives the sense that one simultaneously inhabits the interior and the exterior of the building. In this way, it becomes possible to think of the discrepancies in space as a system.

Through the process of thinking of the *mask* as becoming *surface*, the idea of a new *device* of *ornament* has emerged. This ought to be considered in a separate chapter, but much as the *mask* becomes a decoration for the surface of space, highlighting the discrepancy between surface and space, the mask in fact carries out the same function as surface. *Ornament* has historically been part of human memory, whether as geometrical patterns or as organic calligraphy, and as such it is a shared resource. Accordingly, even as ornament is a complete art form in itself, it also has the capacity to draw people away into another universe through its universality. This is because ornament is already inherently superficial, but is also a structure for guiding people into an understanding of its depth. This kind of ornament, decoratively layered onto the surface of architecture, applies meaning to architectural space, shakes out meaning from surface, and reveals new expression in otherwise static space. The shining moment of speculatively built housing is the *ornament* that covers the facade, bright with reciprocal interference, suggesting a different universe. But in fact that skin is nothing more than an applied image that sparks some resonance with the viewer.

Alongside the development of the International Style in Europe in the 1930s, a style called Art Deco became fashionable; these movements arrived in Japan simultaneously, and carried the same weight of influence for a certain generation of architects. Of course, you can see this merely as the importing of an exuberant movement of modernism, but when it is mixed with the traditional architecture of Japan—a country that was going through changes independently at this time—the resulting hybrid architecture is extremely surface-oriented and decorative. Rather than calling the resultant architecture International Style, it seems more appropriate to call it Art Deco. Architects who began practicing during this period would shoehorn both the traditional Japanese style and the International Style into the design of one house, or engage in the fascinating phenomenon of practicing both styles of architecture at once. These architects were apparently untroubled by the difference between the styles, and a glimpse of mannerist unification can be recognized within that contradiction. Because this architecture is essentially superficial and inherently light, such contradiction doesn't necessarily read as a contradiction.

There isn't really space here to explore this problem fully, but the influence of the surface on spaces without centrality can be read both in modernist constructs and in traditional Japanese structures such as the tea ceremony arbor. In Japanese traditional arts, like the tea ceremony and flower-arranging, there are inherent qualities of front (*hare*) and back (*ke*) that are always observed. The mixing of the two affords an unprecedented type of space, where the natural surface quality is overlaid with a playful hidden character. The interaction of front and back bears some resemblance to the mixing of the *sacred* and the *profane* as unfolded in this essay.

5. Once Again to the City

I started writing this article about a house that I had designed, its distance from the city that surrounds it, and how that distance could be collapsed. This essay deals with space that is the extrapolation of two different worlds—the oppositional worlds of *sacred* space and *profane* space. Architects, while living in the *profane* world, continually yearn for *sacred* spaces. Although in our everyday lives we only have direct access to *profane* space, through ontology we have the tools to apprehend *sacred* space, which we instinctively desire. If we could create a new space through a synthesis of the *sacred* and the *profane*, this space would provide a new path for invigorating architecture. Once we can apprehend that space, architecture could have the opportunity to open up to the city and appropriate the space between itself and its context. Thus it becomes possible to conceive of the *device* of transforming surface. At last the obstinate architect can retreat back into his shell and turn his back on the city, continuing to practice in his ivory tower. In a paradoxical outcome, architecture is isolated from the city.

But, given that, what on earth is the lesson that this generation of architects can pass on to the younger generation of students? In the end, once the dust has settled, what can finally be gleaned from this experiment? Even the terms of the debate have evolved, and at last architecture is breaking free from the dichotomy of universality versus context. I feel that through the specific materials and situation—rather than the concepts—of architecture, elements as fundamental as architecture's structural form have become free. What makes this freedom unique is that, for the first time, architects can tread in the chaotic territory of the formerly untouched city. This is a completely different territory and technique in relation to the city than that which was tested by the architects of the 1960s. The earnest endeavor of the mastermind architect determines how far the reflection of the *sacred* space emerges from its concealment within this *profane* world.

NOTES

1. Koji Taki, "Nakano Honcho no Ie" in Shinkenchiku, 54, no. 2 (1978).

2. Koji Taki, "The Concept of 'Form,'" Shinkenchiku 11 (1976).

3. Kazuhiro Ishii, "Dojidai no kenchikushita-chi," A+U 11 (1977).

4. A conical pit dug in sandy soil by an ant-lion larva. (Translator's note)

5. See, for example, Colin Rowe, Collage City (Cambridge, MA: MIT Press, 1978). (Translator's note)

6. The Romanian historian and University of Chicago professor Mircea Eliade (1907–86) wrote extensively on religion and philosophy. One of his most important writings dealt with splitting the human experience of reality into sacred and profane space and time. See note 7. (Translator's note)

7. Mircea Eliade and Willard R. Trask, The Sacred and the Profane: The Nature of Religion (New York: Harcourt, Brace, 1959).

8. This word refers to a fixed and specific "place," rather than the undifferentiated universal "space" of modernism. (Translator's note)

9. Walter Benjamin, "The Work of Art in the Age of Mechanical Reproduction" (1921), reprinted in Michael William Jennings et al., The Work of Art in the Age of Its Technological Reproducibility, and Other Writings on Media (Cambridge, MA: Belknap Press, 2008), 9–55. (Translator's note)

10. Eliade and Trask, The Sacred and the Profane.

11. Toyo Ito, "Korubyuji'e to to vuenchuri no kosaku suru chiten ni kyo hitotsu no ken-chiku ga seiritsu suru," unpublished, 1978.

12. Akira Yamaguchi, "Center and Periphery in Culture," Sekai (July 1977).

13. Kenzaburo Oe, Shosetsu no hoho (Tokyo: Iwanami Publishing, 1978).

BASE AND SUPERSTRUCTURE IN TOYO ITO

JULIAN WORRALL

In his introduction to a recent collection of translations of Toyo Ito's writing, Thomas Daniell distills the evolution of Ito's thought into four themes, each corresponding to one of the four decades of his career: robot, city, body, and nature. Daniell notes that these represent a "trajectory that suggests a telescoped reversal of the history of human civilization," a kind of inverse teleology culminating in the most primitive ground of existence.[1] The last of these stages, corresponding to the keyword "nature," commences with the construction of the Sendai Mediatheque in 1999, during which Ito experiences what could be described as an epiphany of reality through his direct encounter with the brute materiality of architectural creation. Ito describes this as a "rude awakening" from the dream that had animated the original design—ethereal, transparent spaces for the virtual bodies of the contemporary metropolis that surf and dwell within flows of electronic media—an awakening prompted by his visit to the steel foundry where the massive elements of the building were being fabricated. Ito recalls:

This shift can be seen as an intellectual phase transition, in which the elements that comprise Ito's central architectural concerns change their state but not their essence. Ito's oeuvre, both built and written, has always pursued questions of the relationship between spaces and bodies. Spaces are manifested through imbrications of structures and envelopes; bodies are complex assemblages bearing both perceptual and behavioral dimensions. Varying the weight on each of these terms yields a field of possibilities across which the trajectory of Ito's work can be traced. But beyond his sustained exploration of the interaction of these core elements—an operation that invites a certain hermetic autonomy—Ito has always been acutely sensitive to the broader cultural and historical context in which his inquiries are played out. His essays and explanations continually link observations of phenomena in the broader society and culture to his own research exploring strategies and operations available to an architecture in response. An enduring historical consciousness can be discerned in Ito's architectural thought—an abiding desire to disclose the lineaments of his age through conjunctions of space, matter, and people.

The sight of the workmen battling with all that steel hit me with such a strong material impact. Steelworkers had told me that "steel is a living thing," which sounded like utter nonsense until I actually witnessed those masses of steel stretching and bending with heat: the raw dynamic of real material was much more appealing than any pure, abstract beauty.[2]

From the Iron Cage to the Emergent Grid

The historical imperative that Ito argues must be addressed by architecture today is the atrophying of genuine and credible encounters with the "real" in the contemporary built environment. The "real" here refers to a cluster of referents, including the materiality of physical substance; the corporeal body, with its capacities for sensuality and affect; nature, in all its organic variation and complexity; and emotionally rich encounters with other human beings. In Ito's analysis, these dimensions of embodied experience have been progressively drained of their lifeblood by the homogenizing, standardizing, flattening impulses of modernism. These impulses operate within the "shrink-wrapped" world of the contemporary metropolis, whose spaces have been rendered "neutral, unambiguous, dry, odorless and homogeneous"—akin to convenience store commodities wrapped in cling-film.[3] The architectural metaphor that best captures these attributes is that of the modernist grid—rational, uniform, infinitely extensible—that regulates all space, orders all diversity, and predetermines all possibility. The grid, touchstone of flexibility and egalitarianism for its modernist advocates, is for Ito the iron cage of rationality.[4]

Architecture's urgent task is thus to dismantle this cage. In this quest, of course, Ito is hardly alone. Perhaps the dominant strain of formal exploration in architecture over the past decade has involved the elaboration of non-linear generative languages of form. But Ito's approach is distinctive for its careful and systematic approach to the task. In his work since Sendai, Ito has been feeling his way toward an array of strategies that progressively unshackle and dissolve the modernist grid's domination of architectural structure, form, and envelope, culminating in the spatial method he calls the "emergent grid." This period has been extraordinarily fertile in the diversity of forms produced, yet remarkably coherent in its pursuit of this agenda. The discussion below, weaving Ito's own words with analyses of his works, traces several lines of this inquiry through a number of projects: the Meiso no Mori Crematorium at Kakamigahara (2006); the Tama Art University Library (2007); and, at an elevated level of spatial complexity, the competition proposal for the Ghent Forum for Music, Dance and Visual Culture (2004) and its ultimate realization in the Taichung Metropolitan Opera House (expected completion 2013).

Although the focus here is on these particular works, they should not be considered in isolation from the range of other works of the post-Sendai period. Other lines of inquiry link the pavilion projects at Bruges (2002) and the Serpentine Gallery in London (2002); these find further elaboration at Tod's (2004) and Mikimoto (2005), both commercial buildings on urban sites.

Meanwhile, the faceted polyhedrons developed in 2008 for the Deichman Library competition in Oslo and realized in the Toyo Ito Museum of Architecture at Omishima (2011) explore similar topologies to those of Ghent and Taichung, while using a different formal language. These various lines of inquiry branch and intersect, producing a generative matrix of possibilities that describe extended families of genetically related projects, all seeking in their own ways to escape the alienation of the modernist grid and to foster a liberating rediscovery of architecture's primitive function as the orchestration of spaces and bodies.

Generative Facades and Optimized Surfaces

The restricted scale and program of the pavilion projects at Bruges and the Serpentine give each the character of tightly defined experiments. Ito used them to focus on the relationship between structure and skin. Both buildings were simple boxes in which all architectural content was invested in the enclosing envelope. The key formal challenge they posed was in the elaboration of relationships between mass and void on the exterior of the building that would avoid modernist

doctrines of gridded frames and panel infills. This in turn prompted the secondary question of the generation and expression of pattern and figuration on the facades.

Ito's relationship with creative engineers on these projects has proven crucial in his development of new approaches toward structural expression. His mission to dissolve the stasis of the grid and reveal the inherent dynamism of space found fertile soil in Cecil Balmond's conception of structural arrangements as the momentary "freezing" of fluid lines of forces and his interest in the underlying role of generative algorithms in phenomena of nature.[5] I asked Ito for his thoughts on the relation of structure, skin, and figuration on the facade. He replied:

Until recently the facade was a system that was cut off from the structure. But combining structure with facade again, we were able to render visible the flow of forces. Although this is what I have been thinking for a while, it enables "flowing space" or expresses "organic symbolism" in a new sense. It became possible to use structure on the facade. Of course, we are inspired by structural engineers such as Cecil Balmond and Mutsuro Sasaki: when we work with these structural engineers, we are able to make a significant change to the landscape of the city. This operates differently from previous forms of architectural symbolism—in this approach, people can "feel" nature. Although it may be expressed abstractly, nonetheless one can feel the flows of forces and can express the forces or systems that exist in nature. Architecture can express such kinds of symbols with such an approach.[6]

Structure here becomes a medium for grasping nature directly through the revelation of structural forces. The resulting figuration of the facade becomes an elaboration of patterns that emerge from the interaction of material elements and ordering rules. The formation of such patterning directly mirrors the way complex natural forms emerge from conjunctions of simple principles. For example, the branching members that animate the facade of the Tod's store in Tokyo do not constitute an image, or even an abstraction of the zelkova trees lining the Omotesando boulevard, but rather a manifestation and revelation of their generative essence as structurally rational branching forms. To borrow a formulation from Balmond, pattern is that which links the metaphorical and the concrete.[7]

Ito's initial explorations of the patterning of the building facade's two-dimensional planes gained depth and volume in his Grin Grin Park in Fukuoka (completed in 2005) and, more convincingly, at the Meiso no Mori Crematorium at Kakamigahara (completed in 2006). In the crematorium the dominant element is the undulating roof, a concrete shell that appears to have the character and lightness of a piece of fabric fluttering in the breeze. The engineer in this case was Mutsuro Sasaki, who contributed his methodology of structural optimization by applying repeated passes of a refinement algorithm. This enabled an initial approximation of the desired form to approach its most structurally efficient shape after a number of iterations—a process that internalized the logic of evolutionary change in nature. The organic here no longer describes an external property of formal resemblance to natural things but a quality immanent in the generation of the form itself, apprehended through simulation. Ito describes the significance of this procedure for the design process:

Until we started thinking in this way, the concept of "simulation" was absent amongst structural engineers. For example, at the Serpentine—in which a square appears to be rotating—whether it is rational or not was unknown from the conventional theory. However, through simulation one can test alternative approaches, such as whether the design would benefit from making the rotating pattern bigger or smaller. By repeating these variations many times, and exploring the possibilities, one can identify the best option. Until this approach became possible, architects tended to assert that their proposals were the best possible, and "optimization" as an idea was not yet recognized. In fact, in our usual way of making design decisions we would—after considering various factors—say that if we want to induce a certain behavior, then such-and-such approach would work better than another. But it has now become possible to apply a similar approach to structure. This has been a big change. This was made possible as simulation through computer technology progressed. When we made models of Kakamigahara and Grin Grin, they were digitalized and structural engineers were able to immediately start simulating and pointing out at which specific points improvements were necessary. It became possible for us to run simulations sixty to seventy times without much difficulty: this gave freedom both to structural engineers and to architects.[8]

During the course of creating Kakamigahara, the potential of the flowing, undulating surface as a field for activating occupation became apparent. At the building's opening, the roof surface was made accessible to guests, and the sensational impact of the experience led Ito to implement undulating floors in exhibitions that he was preparing in Tokyo and Berlin. At the New "Real" exhibition in Tokyo, which opened in November 2006, an entire gallery was equipped with a billowing trafficable floor. The liberating effect that this had on visitors to the exhibition (particularly on children) suggested that fluid floor surfaces had a strong potential as shapers of collective occupation and behavior.

At the Tama Art University Library, the grid reappears in warped and distorted guise. The plan resembles a grid, but one in which the lines are curved, establishing

non-uniform spaces and unexpected connections, while the section reveals a honeycomb of arched vaults. The beauty and power of the arch lies in its contraposition of the opposed motifs of weight and buoyancy. Here, the thinness of the walls and the proportions of the arches highlight the latter quality, so that the vaulted spaces seem to hang rather than to press, to the extent that they appear to want to fall skyward on the upper level. At the same time, these spatial effects in depth are subtly undermined by the planar and flattened nature of the spanning walls, deliberately attenuated to a mere 8 inches in thickness. A subtle tension emerges between the spatial effects and the figurative outline.

The facade, by virtue of its inherent tendency toward a surface condition, plays out this tension most visibly. Unlike many of Ito's projects from Sendai onward, in which the question of the facade is resolved through a simple sectional slice at the boundary line, at Tama no arbitrary, external site constraint impinges on the volume. The facade line is established along selected curving lines within the warped grid. This approach strengthens the sense that the building is an element that is carefully selected rather than chopped from a larger field. The facade then becomes a clean diagram of the generative motif: a warped, arched plane.

This pattern was developed from the fluid, stalactite-like columns at the Kakamigahara Crematorium project—fully three-dimensional volumes made of concrete that has been painstakingly applied around a hot-rolled steel pillar. They appear continuous with the rest of the roof. The Tama columns are an "abbreviation" of the ones at Kakamigahara, attenuated to the cruciform generated by the intersection of the dividing planes. Rather than being independent vaulting elements spanning between columnar supports, as in classical configurations, the arches here are extensions of the columns, growing and spreading from junctions in the warped grid like branches unfurling from their stems. The result is a spatial matrix that appears both aerated and rhizomatic, approaching the character of a space-filling foam or marrow. In this design can be found anticipations of its generalization, in the form of the "emergent grid."

The Emergent Grid: The Ghent Forum for Music, Dance and Visual Culture and the Taichung Metropolitan Opera House

Ito's investigations into post-grid techniques for the facade and volume of his buildings achieve their apotheosis in his schemes for the Ghent Forum for Music, Dance and Visual Culture (2004, unrealized) and the Taichung Metropolitan Opera House (competition held in 2005; completion expected in 2013). These schemes propose to house their programs within a porous, sponge-like matrix formed from a continuous manifold of fluidly curving surfaces. Interior and exterior imbricate and interpenetrate the volume in three dimensions. This matrix is conceptually generated from a folded mesh that links gridded planes drawn apart to reveal the manifold. Program elements of various sizes are accommodated by varying the pitch of the grid and the folds of the mesh. In this way, large volumes, such as the two thousand– and eight hundred–seat theaters at Taichung, can be accommodated within the block.

As at Tama, the ghost of the grid is still present in these works, and serves as the geometric origin of the process that leads to the folded spatial matrix. Here, however, the three-dimensional patterns that define the spatial order emerge from a generative process: hence Ito's rendering of it as the "emergent grid." His smoothed polyhedrons are another way of imagining the spatial form's derivation.

Towards an Architecture of Liberation

Lurking in the background of these strenuous efforts to unshackle architecture from the tyranny of the modernist grid is a rhetoric of freedom. This may appear to be a simply formal freedom, a liberation from Cartesian geometric constraints. But Ito has consistently revealed an abiding concern for the behavior and experience of his buildings' inhabitants. Ultimately, underlying Ito's indefatigable efforts to forge a new set of formal operations in architecture is the conviction that they can liberate people from the constrictions of modern environments and reconnect them to the sources of their vitality as living, feeling beings.

The following comments exchanged between Ito (text in purple) and myself (text in black) illustrates Ito's position on the emancipatory powers and purposes of architecture:

Let's talk about freedom. I think you have tried to liberate architecture from the modernist grid. You also said that you want to free people's behavior. So if we talk politically, it seems you are taking the position of a "libertarian." You prioritize freedom.

Yes, I would like to pursue that.

Today, architects in Japan often focus on structure and technique, whereas in the 1960s, they also talked about the political or social aspects of architecture. Why in recent years don't we seem to hear a lot about these other aspects? What kind of position do you take on this?

I think that most architects today are withdrawn. I don't understand why they are withdrawn. At some point, architecture lost its mission to change society. It is largely because architecture has become a tool of capital. But I believe that, limited as it may be, architecture still has a power to propose something to society, or has some role to play in society. The expectation for such a potential is the primary motivation for me to design architecture. When I take up commercial projects such as Tod's and Mikimoto, I think it could be risky. But I want to make people free through the power of architecture. Freedom is not simply a political matter. When people are outside they tend to act freely, but as soon as they are in the space, kids, for example, are told to "behave." Under such a social order, people become controlled. But I believe people still have the capacity to be free.

I like very much the book by [Bernard] Rudofsky that said, "let's lie down and eat."[9] I want to make architecture that allows people to be relaxed—to be eating and reading while lying down, which is getting closer to a natural condition. However, this does not mean the elimination of architecture. The fact that architecture exists is a sign of the existence of human beings. People express their existence through creating art and architecture, although how to prove it in the contemporary context remains an open question.[10]

These questions of the relationship between the spatial and the social or political are once again at the forefront of architectural thought. As the true costs of the neo-liberal deference to the market as the polestar of contemporary societies become apparent, and as public space rediscovers its historical vocation as the crucible of politics after decades of consumption-induced torpor, the question of space as the realm for the elaboration of social goals and human freedom is being posed anew. In his sustained pursuit of an architecture liberated from the rigid geometrical dogmas of modernism, and in his advocacy of meaningful human experiences and encounters grounded in bodily encounters with space, Toyo Ito has, at root, been exploring these precise questions.

Ito's architectural thinking manifests two parallel discourses of "liberation": one, on the plane of architectural orchestration, encompassing spatial arrangements and structural geometries; the other, at the level of social effects, encompassing human activity, relationships, and experiences. These planes stand in conceptual and causal relation to one another. Here it is perhaps productively provocative to deploy an old Marxist vocabulary—of "base" and "superstructure"—to these levels of Ito's thought.[11] In Marx's conception, material relations of production form the foundation, or "base," of society, from which ideological and social phenomena emerge and are supported. Changes in this base lead to corresponding changes in the superstructure. In a double translation, where an architectural metaphor becomes a model of social process and thence returns bearing political resonance to an architectural context, Ito's emergent grid can be seen as the formal foundation for building a new superstructure of human behavior and perception. In this, the true vocation of Toyo Ito the architect is revealed—a vocation that remains as committed to the ideal of human freedom as the high modernists believed they were.

Post-3.11 Postscript

A deep concern for the public role and understanding of architecture has long been a significant part of Ito's stance, but it is perhaps in Ito's response to Japan's devastating disaster of March 11, 2011, that the ultimate goals of his patient quest are most clearly discernible. As part of "Kishin no Kai," a group of five prominent architects (the others are Riken Yamamoto, Hiroshi Naito, Kengo Kuma, and Kazuyo Sejima), Ito and his comrades have sought to employ architectural intelligence to contribute to the post-disaster relief and reconstruction efforts. One of the immediate fruits of this effort is the "Home for All" (*Minna-no-Ie*) project. This project seeks to build community spaces for victims of the disaster housed in prefabricated temporary housing that, in Ito's words, "is no different from a prison."[12] Ito set out to erect a modest timber structure along traditional lines for communal dining and conversation, complete with earthen floors, tatami mats, and wood-burning stoves. He describes the building of this structure and the overwhelmingly positive reception it has received from its users as "the most satisfying experience of building I have ever had,"even raising doubts about the purpose and meaning of architectural innovation.[13] Yet it comes as no surprise that with this humble "home for all," this most inventive of architects and most committed of liberators would find his deepest fulfillment.

1. Thomas Daniell, "The Fugitive," in Toyo Ito, Tarzans in the Media Forest and Other Essays, trans. and ed. Thomas Daniell (London: AA Publications, 2010), 15.

2. Toyo Ito, "Dynamic Delight over Aesthetic Purity" (2002), in Ito, Tarzans in the Media Forest, 160.

3. This perspective is elaborated in Ito's essay "Architectural Scenery in the Saran Wrap City," in Ito, Tarzans in the Media Forest, 92–99.

4. The metaphor is, of course, Max Weber's, from The Protestant Ethic and the Spirit of Capitalism (originally published as a series of essays, in German, in 1904–5). Ito's diagnosis of the environments of modernity has strong resonance with Weber's analysis of the systems of bureaucratic standardization and the "disenchantment of the world" in advanced capitalist societies.

5. See, for example, Cecil Balmond, Informal (Munich: Prestel, 2002), 166–71, for one statement of this perception.

6. Toyo Ito, in conversation with the author, Tokyo, August 15, 2011.

7. Cecil Balmond, Element (Munich: Prestel, 2008), 160.

8. Ito, in conversation with the author.

9. Bernard Rudofsky, Now I Lay Me Down to Eat: Notes and Footnotes on the Lost Art of Living (New York: Doubleday, 1980).

10. Ito, in conversation with the author.

11. Here I refer to the terms as introduced by Karl Marx in his A Contribution to the Critique of Political Economy, originally published, in German, in 1859.

12. Remarks given to visiting student group from Strelka Institute for Media, Architecture, and Design, Tokyo, December 2, 2011.

13. Ibid.

PICTURING "HOME FOR ALL" 2011

TOYO ITO

WITH

RIKEN YAMAMOTO
HIROSHI NAITO
KENGO KUMA
KAZUYO SEJIMA

A CALL FOR DESIGN SUBMISSIONS,
SUMMER 2011

The massive March 11 earthquake and tsunami wrought unprecedented damage in northeastern Japan. Over 100,000 people lost their homes and were forced to take shelter in relief centers and temporary housing.

The relief centers offer no privacy and scarcely enough room to stretch out and sleep, while the hastily tacked-up temporary housing units are little more than rows of empty shells: grim living conditions either way. Yet even under such harsh conditions, people try to smile and make do, using empty boxes for dining tables, staging amateur concerts in cramped quarters. They gather to share and communicate even in extreme circumstances—a moving vision of community at its most basic. Likewise, what we see here are very origins of architecture, the minimal shaping of communal spaces. An architect is someone who can make such places for meager meals show a little more humanity, make them a little more beautiful, a little more comfortable.

I would call such primal architecture *Minna-no-Ie* ("Home for All"), communal gathering places we can build in the disaster areas in between the relief centers and temporary housing. The idea is to make something like a house that is all living room and no bedrooms. A place with sofas and tables where people can go to sit and talk, maybe read a book or newspaper over coffee. A reassuring place that offers a bit of normal life. No matter how humble and unassuming, to those who have lost their own home, the "Home for All" might just afford a viable temporary solution.

For the time being, let's consider our "Home for All" a one-off gesture, but one that, as recovery efforts proceed, just might lead to more permanent structures. We might be encouraging a whole new direction in creative community architecture.

I'm calling on people around the world to draw up and submit images of the "Home for All" to benefit and encourage those in the disaster areas. Architects and aspiring students of architecture, even children and disaster victims, let's see your "Home for All" ideas so we can start building a back-to-the-basics future from the ground up.

桜の下の まん幕から「みんなのいえ」へ

人はすべてを失っても
集い、飲み、食べ、語り合う.

Toyolto
03 July 2011

COLLECTIONS OF ESSAYS BY TOYO ITO

In English

Tarzans in the Media Forest and Other Essays. Translated and edited by Thomas Daniell. London: AA Publications, 2010.

Toyo Ito: Works, Projects, Writings. Edited by Andrea Maffei. London: Electa, 2006.

Toyo Ito: Blurring Architecture, 1971–2005. Edited by Ulrich Schneider and Marc Feustel. Milan: Charta, 1999.

In Japanese

Toso suru Kenchiku. Tokyo: Seidosha, 2000.

Kaze no Henyotai: Kenchiku Kuronikuru. Tokyo: Seidosha, 1989.

VOLUMES ILLUSTRATING THE WORK OF TOYO ITO

Ito, Toyo, Dana Buntrock, and Taro Igarashi. Toyo Ito. London: Phaidon, 2009.

Ito, Toyo, and Fernando Márquez Cecilia. Toyo Ito: 2005–2009. Liquid Space. Madrid: El Croquis, 2009.

Ito, Toyo, and Koji Taki. Toyo Ito: 2001–2005. Beyond Modernism. Madrid: El Croquis, 2005.

Ito, Toyo. Toyo Ito: 1986–1995. Madrid: El Croquis, 1995.

CONTRIBUTORS

TOYO ITO

Toyo Ito is an internationally renowned architect. A student in the 1960s, Ito founded his own studio in Tokyo in 1971. Since then, he has consistently produced works of striking inventiveness, such as Tod's Omotesando and Sendai Mediatheque, which explore the dynamic relationship between buildings and their environments.

Over decades of practice, Ito has developed a design approach that focuses on freeing architecture from the grid system, which he believes homogenizes not only the urban landscape but also the lives of the people who inhabit it. His recent projects include a library for the Tama Art University, where Ito holds a teaching position, and the Taichung Metropolitan Opera House, which is currently under construction.

The architect's built work has been published in numerous volumes, including a series of books by El Croquis and a recent monograph by Phaidon. His essays have appeared in a variety of international journals and are collected in books, published both in his native Japanese and in translation. Ito is an honorary fellow of the AIA and RIBA, and has numerous awards to his credit, including the RIBA 2006 Royal Gold Medal.

STAN ALLEN

Stan Allen is an architect and George Dutton '27 Professor at the Princeton University School of Architecture, where he served as dean from 2002 to 2012. His buildings and projects have been published in Points and Lines: Diagrams and Projects for the City (1999) and his essays are collected in Practice: Architecture, Technique and Representation (2008). His most recent book is the edited volume <u>Landform Building: Architecture's New Terrain</u>, published by Lars Müller in 2011. Allen lectures extensively in the United States and abroad and participates regularly in international design conferences and symposia.

JESSIE TURNBULL

Jessie Turnbull is an architect practicing in New York City. After receiving her Bachelor of Arts in Architecture at the University of Cambridge, she spent two years in Tokyo as a scholar of the Daiwa Anglo Japanese Foundation, studying Japanese and working for the architecture firm Atelier Bow-Wow. She completed her graduate studies in architecture at the Princeton University School of Architecture, where for three years she also served as an editor of <u>Pidgin</u> magazine.

JULIAN WORRALL

Julian Worrall is an assistant professor at the Institute for Advanced Study, Waseda University, in Tokyo. He received his doctorate from the University of Tokyo in 2005. His dissertation is entitled "Railway Urbanism: Commuter Rail and the Production of Public Space in Twentieth-Century Tokyo." He is a contributing writer for numerous professional journals and newspapers worldwide, including <u>Domus</u>, <u>Icon</u>, <u>Mark</u>, and the <u>Japan Times</u>. His <u>Twenty-first Century Tokyo: A Guide to Contemporary Architecture</u>, coauthored with Erez Golani-Solomon, was published in 2009.

ILLUSTRATIONS

142

All images of projects, buildings, and models were kindly provided by Toyo Ito and Associates except where noted.

Published by
Princeton Architectural Press
37 East Seventh Street
New York, New York 10003

Visit our website at www.papress.com.

Toyo Ito, "The Reflection of the *Sacred* in the *Profane* World" was originally
published in Japanese in *Shinkenchiku* 06 (1980): © Shinkenchiku, 1980.
Used with permission. Translation © Jessie Turnbull, 2012.

Kassler Series Editor: Stan Allen
Managing Editor, SoA Books: Nancy Eklund Later
Project Editor, Princeton Architectural Press: Megan Carey
Design: Omnivore

Princeton Architectural Press extends special thanks to:
Bree Anne Apperley, Sara Bader, Nicola Bednarek Brower, Janet Behning,
Fannie Bushin, Carina Cha, Andrea Chlad, Russell Fernandez, Will Foster,
Jan Haux, Diane Levinson, Jennifer Lippert, Jacob Moore, Gina Morrow,
Katharine Myers, Margaret Rogalski, Elana Schlenker, Dan Simon, Sara
Stemen, Andrew Stepanian, Paul Wagner, and Joseph Weston of Princeton
Architectural Press —Kevin C. Lippert, publisher

Library of Congress Cataloging-in-Publication Data
Toyo Ito : forces of nature / Jessie Turnbull, editor. — 1st ed.
143 p. : ill. (chiefly col.) ; 21 cm. — (The Kassler Lectures)
"April 15, 2009."
Includes bibliographical references.
ISBN 978-1-61689-101-5 (pbk. : alk. paper)
1. Ito, Toyo, 1941—Criticism and interpretation. 2. Architecture, Modern—
21st century. I. Turnbull, Jessie, 1983— II. Title: Forces of nature.

NA1559.I84T69 2012
720.92—dc23
                                2012013636